PASSTRAK®

Life and Health Insurance

Questions and Answers

5th Edition

Dearborn™
Financial Services
A **Kaplan Professional** Company

This publication is designed to provide accurate and authoritative information in regard to the subject matter covered. It is sold with the understanding that the publisher is not engaged in rendering legal, accounting or other professional service. If legal advice or other expert assistance is required, the services of a competent professional person should be sought.

This text is updated periodically to reflect changes in laws and regulations. To verify that you have the most recent edition, you may call DEARBORN at 1-800-423-4723.

Fourth printing, February 2003

ISBN: 0-7931-4851-0

INTRODUCTION

For nine years, *PASSTRAK® Life and Health Insurance Questions & Answers* has helped candidates successfully prepare for state insurance licensing examinations. Research has proven that the best way to prepare for an objective exam is to take similar practice exams. In so doing, the student can discover weak areas that may require additional study and will gain confidence in his or her test-taking ability. Because this book provides solid and efficient exam preparation, it is an indispensable final step before taking the licensing examination.

PASSTRAK® Life and Health Insurance Questions & Answers contains more than 650 multiple-choice questions in three parts: Principles of Life and Health Insurance, Principles of Life Insurance and Principles of Health Insurance. This organization allows the student to concentrate on life insurance or health insurance or both, depending on the exam he or she plans to take. The style, scope and format of the questions contained in this book are distinctly similar to the licensing exams conducted and administered by Assessment Systems, Inc. (ASI), Experior or by your state insurance department. Each chapter opens with a list of the various concepts covered by the questions in that chapter. The questions are organized to follow the outline sequence; therefore, a student can readily identify topic or concept areas that require further study or review.

Each chapter concludes with answers and detailed rationales. The explanations are key to effective self-study and review and will also help pinpoint subject areas where the student is weak.

The emphasis of the material in this book is directed to subjects common to all life and health insurance licensing exams, regardless of the state or the testing organization. However, the student should note that this book does *not* contain questions dealing with specific state laws and regulations, as they vary from state to state.

PASSTRAK® Life and Health Insurance Questions & Answers can be studied regardless of the text or class the student used to learn insurance. We wish you success in your career. Conscientious study on your part will help assure you of a good beginning. Good luck.

TABLE OF CONTENTS

Part One

Principles of Life and Health Insurance

Basic Principles of Life and Health Insurance

1. With regard to insurance, risk can be defined as

    A. certainty regarding loss
    B. uncertainty regarding loss
    C. uncertainty regarding financial gain
    D. certainty regarding financial gain

2. The risk that involves the chance of both loss and gain is

    A. pure risk
    B. impure risk
    C. speculative risk
    D. whole risk

3. All of the following statements pertaining to risk are correct EXCEPT F

    T A. pure risk involves only the chance of loss; there is never a possibility of gain or profit
    T B. uncertainty regarding financial loss is the definition of risk; therefore, it is characteristic of both pure and speculative risks
    F C. a stock market venture is an example of a pure risk
    T D. only pure risks are insurable

4. Which of the following risks is insurable?

    A. Pure risks
    B. Speculative risks
    C. Whole risks
    D. Partial risks

5. Self-insurance is an example of what kind of risk treatment?

    A. Avoidance
    B. Reduction
    C. Retention
    D. Transference

6. Treating risk by purchasing insurance is an example of

    A. avoiding risk
    B. transferring risk
    C. reducing risk
    D. retaining risk

7. All forms of insurance are alike in all of the following ways EXCEPT F

    A. all are based on the law of large numbers
    B. all are implemented through a contractual agreement between the insurance owner and insurer
    C. the nature of the perils covered is the same
    D. all indemnify financial loss

8. Alcoholism is an example of a

    A. peril
    B. physical hazard
    C. moral hazard
    D. morale hazard

9. Which of the following statements BEST summarizes the function of insurance?

    A. It is a form of legalized gambling.
    B. It spreads financial risk over a large group so as to minimize the loss to any one individual.
    C. It protects against living too long.
    D. It spreads financial risk over a diverse group of people who are exposed to different risks.

10. The law of large numbers states that

    A. the smaller the number of risks combined into one group, the less uncertainty there will be as to the amount of loss that will be incurred
    B. the larger the number of risks combined into one group, the less uncertainty there will be as to the amount of loss that will be incurred
    C. the smaller the number of risks combined into one group, the larger the loss will be to any one individual in that group
    D. the larger the number of risks combined into one group, the smaller the loss will be to any one individual in that group

11. Assume there are four different mortality tables. Of these, the most reliable would be the mortality table covering

    A. 100,000 lives
    B. 500,000 lives
    C. 4,000,000 lives
    D. 10,000,000 lives

12. All of the following are elements of an insurable risk EXCEPT

    A. the loss must be due to chance
    B. the loss must be predictable
    C. the loss must be catastrophic
    D. the loss must have a determinable value

13. The amount of money an insurer sets away to pay future claims is called the

    A. premium
    B. reserve
    C. dividend
    D. accumulated interest

14. Which of the following constitutes an insurable interest?

    A. The policyowner must expect to benefit from the insured's death.
    B. The policyowner must expect to suffer a loss when the insured dies or becomes disabled.
    C. The beneficiary, by definition, has an insurable interest in the insured.
    D. The insured must have a personal or business relationship with the beneficiary.

15. With regard to life insurance, all of the following statements are correct EXCEPT

    A. all individuals are considered to have insurable interests in themselves
    B. spouses are automatically considered to have insurable interests in each other
    C. a creditor has an insurable interest in a debtor
    D. insurable interest must be maintained throughout the life of the contract

16. In order to be insured, a group must be randomly selected in order to avoid

    A. chance of loss
    B. catastrophic loss
    C. adverse selection
    D. increase in premium

17. Suppose a life insurance company is organized in Detroit where it maintains its home office. In Michigan, the company is classified as a

    A. domestic company
    B. local company
    C. foreign company
    D. preferred company

18. Which term correctly describes a life insurance company that has been organized outside the United States or its possessions?

    A. Foreign
    B. Alien
    C. Remote
    D. Distant

19. A life insurance company organized in Pennsylvania, with its home office in Philadelphia, is licensed to conduct business in New York. In New York, this company is classified as a(n)

    A. domestic company
    B. alien company
    C. foreign company
    D. regional company

20. Which of the following statements pertaining to life insurance companies is CORRECT?

    A. If a certain life insurance company is owned by its policyowners, it is a stock company.
    B. The primary purpose of a life insurance company that is organized as a stock company is to earn a profit for its stockholders.
    C. A stock company that issues both participating and nonparticipating life insurance policies is classified as a full-lines company.
    D. Mutual insurance companies sell insurance to insurers.

21. An insurance company that is owned by its policyowners is known as a

    A. stock insurance company
    B. mutual life insurance company
    C. parent company
    D. domestic company

22. All of the following statements about participating policies are correct EXCEPT

    A. they are only issued by stock companies
    B. the annual premium rate is generally higher than that for nonparticipating policies
    C. they enable the policyowner to share in the earnings of the company
    D. they are eligible for dividends

23. The term "mutualization" refers to

    A. dissolution of an insurance company
    B. transferring control of a company from policyowners to stockholders
    C. sharing company profits with stockholders
    D. transferring control of a company from stockholders to policyowners

24. A stock company that issues both participating and nonparticipating policies is classified as a(n)

    A. all-lines company
    B. blended company
    C. mixed company
    D. combined company

25. An advance premium assessable mutual company

    A. is a stock company
    B. assesses each member for his or her portion of the losses that actually occur
    C. is owned by its stockholders
    D. charges a premium at the beginning of the policy period

26. In order to qualify as a fraternal benefit society, an organization must have all of the following EXCEPT

    A. a lodge system
    B. ritualistic work
    C. a representative form of government
    D. a large sales force

27. All of the following may be classified as service organizations EXCEPT a

    A. health insurance company
    B. health maintenance organization
    C. Blue Cross/Blue Shield organization
    D. preferred provider organization

28. Which of the following organizations contracts with select doctors and hospitals to be a health care provider for its members?

    A. HMO
    B. PPO
    C. MIB
    D. DPO

29. Health maintenance organizations are known for stressing

    A. preventive medicine and early treatment
    B. state-sponsored health care plans
    C. in-hospital care and services
    D. health care services for government employees

30. Under what system do a group of doctors and hospitals in a designated area contract with an insurer to provide services at a prearranged cost to the insured?

    A. HMO
    B. PPO
    C. MIB
    D. DPO

31. A group of individuals who agree to share each others' losses is known as a

    A. mixed group
    B. reciprocal exchange
    C. reinsurer
    D. service organization

32. An insurer of an insurer is known as a

    A. mixed group
    B. reciprocal
    C. reinsurer
    D. service organization

33. All of the following are examples of social insurance EXCEPT

    A. Social Security
    B. Medicare
    C. Blue Cross and Blue Shield coverage
    D. workers' compensation

34. With regard to medical benefits available through the federal government, Medicaid provides

    A. medical benefits exclusively for the aged
    B. funds to states to assist their medical public assistance programs
    C. medical benefits for the disabled, regardless of income
    D. medical benefits to all who have contributed to its funding through payroll taxes

35. All of the following benefits are available under Social Security EXCEPT

    A. death benefits
    B. old-age benefits
    C. disability benefits
    D. medical expense benefits

36. Under Social Security, a fully insured worker is eligible for

    A. disability benefits only
    B. retirement, death and survivor benefits
    C. death benefits only
    D. survivor benefits only

37. Under Social Security, a worker's primary insurance amount (PIA) is

    A. a total of benefits received during the first year of retirement
    B. an amount equal to the worker's full retirement benefit at the full retirement age or disability benefit
    C. the amount his or her surviving spouse will receive upon the worker's death
    D. larger than the combined insurance benefit payable to the worker and spouse at age 62

38. Lee has a Social Security PIA of $800 at the time of his death. How much is payable to his surviving spouse as a lump-sum death benefit under Social Security?

    A. $0
    B. $255
    C. $500
    D. $800

39. All of the following statements about Servicemembers' and Veterans' Group Life insurance are correct EXCEPT

    A. the Veterans' Group Life Insurance (VGLI) program offers service members leaving active duty a means by which to convert their Servicemembers' Group Life Insurance policies to 5-year term policies.
    B. the Servicemembers' Group Life are term policies available to all active members of the military.
    C. Servicemembers' Group Life and Veterans' Group Life policies are issued by the government.
    D. Servicemembers' Group Life insurance remains effective 120 days following discharge from the service.

40. Social Security benefits are financed by a special tax paid by

    A. employers as a percentage of their profits
    B. state and local governments
    C. business, based on the amount of their assets
    D. employees, employers and those who are self-employed

41. For Social Security purposes, the Average Indexed Monthly Earnings (AIME) is based on an individual's

    A. average indexed monthly earnings
    B. lifetime earnings history
    C. average of five years of highest income earned
    D. any five-year period of uninterrupted work

42. Ron is eligible for full death, retirement and disability benefits under Social Security. His work status is

    A. completely insured
    B. currently insured
    C. fully insured
    D. partially insured

43. Self-insurance is

    A. insurance written by an insurer on itself
    B. practiced by organizations that establish reserves to protect themselves against loss
    C. illegal in many states
    D. available through the federal government

44. In an insurance transaction, who does a licensed agent legally represent?

    A. Insurer
    B. Applicant
    C. State insurance department
    D. National Association of Insurance Commissioners

45. An individual appointed by an insurer to administer its business in a given territory is called a

    A. general agent
    B. special agent
    C. broker
    D. career agent

46. A field representative who works between the insurance company's central office and the agency force in his or her territory is a

    A. general agent
    B. special agent
    C. broker
    D. career agent

47. Which of the following statements pertaining to agents and brokers is CORRECT?

    A. A "contract of agency" defines the authority of a broker.
    B. An agent may not be held legally responsible for actions not authorized by his or her company.
    C. Technically, a broker represents the client in an insurance transaction.
    D. A broker who places business with multiple companies needs only one broker's contract.

48. An agent represents his or her company in all of the following ways EXCEPT

    A. the agent solicits applications for insurance
    B. the agent describes the company's policies to prospects
    C. the agent collects premiums from applicants and policyowners
    D. the agent searches for the least expensive insurance for a consumer

49. Agency law encompasses all of the following EXCEPT

    A. The acts of an agent are the acts of the principal.
    B. A contract completed by the agent on behalf of the principal is a contract of the principal.
    C. Knowledge of the principal is knowledge of the agent.
    D. Payments made to an agent intended for the principal are payments made to the principal.

50. All of the following are agent responsibilities toward the applicant EXCEPT

    A. explaining the coverage
    B. delivering the policy
    C. prepaying the initial premium
    D. collecting the initial premium

51. The authority that an insurer gives to its agents by means of the agent's contract is known as

    A. express authority
    B. implied authority
    C. fiduciary responsibility
    D. general authority

52. The term for an individual who occupies a position of trust when handling the financial affairs of another is

    A. fiduciary
    B. trustee
    C. superior
    D. consultant

53. An agent in the XYZ Insurance Company, equipped with business cards, sample XYZ policies and an XYZ rate book, informs a prospect that XYZ has given him unlimited binding authority. The prospect assumes this is true. Given the prospect's assumption, which of the following correctly defines the agent's authority in this case?

    A. Express authority
    B. Implied authority
    C. Apparent authority
    D. Binding authority

54. Insurers that deal directly with insureds without the use of agents are known as

    A. independent insurers
    B. direct writers
    C. mass marketers
    D. reciprocals

55. Which of the following statements regarding mass marketing insurance is CORRECT?

    A. It takes advantage of small group situations.
    B. It is considered unethical and has been outlawed in some states.
    C. It involves one-on-one meetings between prospects and agents.
    D. It is marketed through various forms of print, visual and aural media.

56. What factor in life insurance is comparable to the morbidity factor in health insurance?

    A. Loading
    B. Mortality
    C. Premium
    D. Interest

57. Assume lightning strikes a home and starts a fire that destroys the structure and its contents. By insurance definition, the fire is the

    A. risk
    B. hazard
    C. peril
    D. proximate cause

58. In an insurance transaction, a broker represents the

    A. insurer
    B. applicant
    C. state insurance department
    D. general public

Answers & Rationale

1. B.   Risk refers to the uncertainty of financial loss. Insurance replaces the uncertainty of risk with certain guarantees of financial stability.
QID: 1000

2. C.   Speculative risk involves the chance of both loss and gain. For example, the placement of a bet at a racetrack is a speculative risk.
QID: 1001

3. C.   A stock market venture involves the chance of both gain and loss and is, therefore, a speculative risk. Pure risk involves only the chance of loss.
QID: 1002

4. A.   Only pure risks are insurable since they involve the chance of loss only.
QID: 1003

5. C.   Self-insurance is a form of risk retention because the individual personally retains the risk and must accept the economic loss if the risk becomes a reality.
QID: 1004

6. B.   Purchasing insurance is the most common method of transferring risk. The burden of carrying the risk and indemnifying the financial or economic loss is transferred from the individual to the insurance company through the insurance contract.
QID: 1005

7. C.   The major difference between life insurance and other forms of insurance is that life insurance covers a certain risk—death—whereas the others insure against contingencies that may or may not happen sickness, fire or theft. The only uncertainty about the risk of death is when it will take place.
QID: 1006

8. C.   A peril is the specific event causing loss. A hazard is any factor that gives rise to a peril. A moral hazard is a subjective characteristic of the insured that increases the chance of loss.
QID: 1007

9. B.   The function of insurance is to safeguard against financial loss by having the losses of a few paid by the contributions of many who are exposed to the same risk.
QID: 1008

10. B.   The law of large numbers operates under the principle that the larger the number of similar risks combined into one group, the less uncertainty there will be as to the amount of loss that group will incur. Thus, an insurance company is able to determine in advance the approximate number of claims it will receive in a given time period for a given risk and place its business on a nonspeculative basis.
QID: 1009

11. D.   The larger the group, the more certain or reliable will be the amount of loss (which, in this case, is the death or mortality rate).
QID: 1010

12. C.   One of the criteria for an insurable risk is that it not be catastrophic. A principle of insurance holds that only a small portion of a given group will experience loss at any one time. Risks that would adversely affect large numbers of people or large amounts of property, such as wars or floods, are typically not insurable.
QID: 1011

13. B.   Reserves can be defined as the amounts that are set aside to fulfill the insurance company's obligation to pay future claims.
QID: 1012

14. B.   Insurable interest requires that the policyowner be expected to benefit from the insured's continuing to live or enjoying good health or to suffer a loss when the insured dies or is disabled.

An insurable interest must exist between the applicant and the insured. It does not need to exist between the applicant and the beneficiary.
QID: 1013

15.   D.   Insurable interest is required only when a contract is issued. It does not have to be maintained throughout the life of the contract nor is it necessary at the time of a claim.
QID: 1014

16.   C.   Adverse selection exists when an insurer has more bad risks than good, resulting in a group of policyowners whose mortality or morbidity experience exceeds the normal or expected rates.
QID: 1015

17.   A.   A domestic insurer is incorporated in the same state in which it sells insurance.
QID: 1016

18.   B.   An alien company is one that is incorporated or organized under the laws of any foreign nation, province or territory.
QID: 1017

19.   C.   A foreign company operates within a state in which it is not chartered and in which its home office is not located.
QID: 1018

20.   B.   Stock companies are owned by stockholders, not policyowners, and they are organized for the purpose of making a profit for their stockholders.
QID: 1019

21.   B.   A mutual life insurance company is a corporation, but there are no stockholders. Instead, the company is owned by its policyowners, from whom its resources are derived. Its assets and income are held for the benefit of the policyowners who, as contractual creditors, have the right to vote for directors or trustees.
QID: 1020

22.   A.   Participating policies are issued by both stock and mutual companies. They are called "participating" because they are eligible for dividends, thus enabling policyowners to share in the earnings of the company. For this reason, the premium cost is generally higher for participating policies than nonparticipating policies.
QID: 1021

23.   D.   "Mutualization" is the term used to describe the process whereby a stock company (one owned by stockholders) becomes a mutual company (one owned by policyowners) through the transfer of control from stockholders to policyowners. Conversely, demutualization occurs when control switches to stockholders from policyowners.
QID: 1022

24.   C.   Stock companies generally sell nonparticipating policies. Mutual companies generally sell participating policies. When a company sells both, it is known as a mixed company.
QID: 1023

25.   D.   Most mutual companies are categorized as advance premium assessable mutual companies and charge a premium in advance, at the beginning of the policy period.
QID: 1024

26.   D.   Noted for their benevolent and charitable activities, fraternal societies are nonprofit organizations that operate for the benefit of their memberships. To retain their tax-exempt status, fraternals must have a lodge system that includes ritualistic work and operate under a representative (elected) form of government.
QID: 1025

27.   A.   Service organizations offer health insurance and health care services. A health insurance company sells only health insurance and not health care services.
QID: 1026

28. A. A health maintenance organization (HMO) contracts with select doctors and hospitals to be a health care provider for its members. Enrollees in the HMO receive services for a fixed premium paid in advance.
QID: 1027

29. A. HMOs stress preventive medicine and early treatment, including routine physicals and visits to doctors.
QID: 1028

30. B. Preferred provider organizations (PPOs) are groups of doctors and hospitals that contract with an insurer to provide services at a prearranged cost, thus allowing insureds to choose among these groups.
QID: 1029

31. B. A reciprocal or reciprocal exchange is an unincorporated mutual organized for the mutual protection of its members.
QID: 1030

32. C. A reinsurer insures part of the life insurance underwritten by another life insurance company to reduce the possible large loss of the latter.
QID: 1031

33. C. Social insurance is provided by the federal and state governments and includes Social Security (death, old-age and disability benefits), Medicare, Medicaid and workers' compensation. Blue Cross and Blue Shield are examples of service insurers.
QID: 1032

34. B. Medicaid provides funds to states to assist their medical public assistance programs. Medicare provides health benefits for the aged and disabled.
QID: 1033

35. D. Social Security provides death benefits, old-age (retirement) benefits and disability benefits to eligible workers.
QID: 1034

36. B. To be eligible for death, retirement and disability benefits, a worker must be fully insured, which means that the worker has earned 40 credits or worked about 10 years under Social Security.
QID: 1035

37. B. Primary insurance amount (PIA) is the amount equal to a worker's full retirement benefit at the full retirement age or his or her disability benefit. Benefits are reduced if a worker retires before age 65.
QID: 1036

38. B. The Social Security lump-sum death benefit is a one-time-only payment of $255 to a deceased worker's surviving spouse or eligible children.
QID: 1037

39. C. Both SGLI and VGLI are issued by private commercial insurers who participate in the programs.
QID: 1038

40. D. Employees, employers and those who are self-employed pay taxes to finance Social Security benefits. These taxes are based on the tax rate (which changes periodically) and an employee's earnings.
QID: 1039

41. B. An individual's retirement benefit is based on his or her Primary Insurance Amount (PIA). To calculate one's PIA, it is necessary to know one's Average Indexed Monthly Earnings (AIME), which is based on an individual's lifetime earnings history. A worker who is born on or after 1938 will use one method of calculation. A worker born before 1938 will use a different one.
QID: 1040

42. C. Fully insured is a status of complete eligibility that provides benefits for retirement, disability and death. A worker who is currently insured is not eligible for all Social Security insurance benefits.
QID: 1041

43. B. Self-insurance is a legitimate method of insuring loss by establishing one's own reserve of funds.
QID: 1042

44. A. Under the law of agency, agents represent insurers.
QID: 1043

45. A. A life and health general agent is an individual appointed by an insurer to administer its business in a given territory. The individual is responsible for building his or her own agency and field force.
QID: 1044

46. B. Special agents work between a home office and the agency force. They are often called upon to resolve problems in the field.
QID: 1045

47. C. An agent represents a company while a broker represents a client. An agent may be held liable for acts beyond his or her authority if the public can reasonably assume he or she has authority for those acts. A contract of agency defines the authority of an agent. A broker is required to have a broker's contract with every company for whom he or she does business.
QID: 1046

48. D. An agent is authorized to solicit applications, describe the company's policies to prospects and potential clients, collect premiums and render service to both prospects and existing clients.
QID: 1047

49. C. A fundamental rule of agency law states that information known to the agent is also known by the principal, as long as the agency relationship exists. Information known to the principal, however, is not presumed to be known to the agent.
QID: 1048

50. C. The agent has no responsibility to pay a client's premium, in advance or at any other time.
QID: 1049

51. A. Express authority is what the insurer intends to, and in fact does, give to its agent through means of the agent's contract. This authority explicitly appoints the agent to act on behalf of the insurer.
QID: 1050

52. A. A fiduciary is an individual occupying a position of trust and confidence when handling or supervising the funds or the affairs of another. A trustee is a person appointed or required by law to execute a trust to the benefit or use of another.
QID: 1051

53. C. Apparent authority is what a third party (such as a member of the public) assumes an agent has, based on the actions or words of the principal. By supplying the agent with business cards, sample policies and rate books, the insurance company has given the impression that it supports the words and actions of its agent.
QID: 1052

54. B. A large volume of insurance is sold through direct writing companies that do not use agents, but instead employ their own salespersons.
QID: 1053

55. D. Mass marketing insurance takes advantage of large group situations, selling through direct mail, newspapers, radio and television. It is an acceptable means of marketing insurance, though there is usually little client contact with an agent or broker.
QID: 1054

56. B. The morbidity factor of the incidence of disability due to accident or sickness at various ages is to health insurance what the mortality factor (incidence of death) is to life insurance.
QID: 1623

57. C. A peril is the immediate specific event causing loss and giving rise to risk. When a building burns, fire is the peril.
QID: 3298

58. B. A Brokers, unlike agents, legally represent the insured and do not have the legal authority to bind the insurer. Brokers solicit and accept applications for insurance and then place the coverage with an insurer.
QID: 3299

2

Uses of Life and Health Insurance

1. Which of the following statements pertaining to the late Dr. S.S. Huebner's human life value concept is CORRECT?

    A. A human life value may be determined by discounting a person's future net earnings for family purposes at a reasonable rate of interest.
    B. A person's total estimated earnings at age 65, plus estimated Social Security benefits for a 10-year period, represent a human life value.
    C. A human life value is equal to the sum of an individual's current earnings.
    D. The value of a human life is calculated by subtracting an individual's debts from his or her annual income.

2. Human life value can be expressed as a(n)

    A. economic factor
    B. priceless commodity
    C. unit of productivity
    D. dollar valuation

3. All of the following usually are included in a final expense fund when determining life insurance needs of a family EXCEPT

    A. last illness and funeral costs
    B. outstanding debts
    C. funds to pay off a mortgage
    D. unpaid federal and state taxes

4. When does a surviving family have the GREATEST need for income?

    A. During the final illness of the death of the breadwinner
    B. While the children are growing up
    C. After the children are independent
    D. During the surviving spouse's old age

5. With regard to a breadwinner's death, the blackout period generally can be defined as

    A. the period during which children are living at home and dependent
    B. the period from when the youngest child is grown to the surviving parent's retirement age
    C. a time when life insurance rarely is needed
    D. the period from the surviving spouse's retirement to death

6. Which of the following terms refers to that period following the death of a breadwinner during which the children are living at home?

    A. Blackout period
    B. Child-rearing period
    C. Provision period
    D. Dependency period

7. Which of the following statements pertaining to sole proprietor buy-sell plans is CORRECT?

    A. Concerning disposition of the business at his or her death, the only alternatives open to a sole proprietor are to dissolve the business or leave it to an heir as a bequest.
    B. A buy-sell agreement for a sole proprietor can be drafted by the proprietor or his or her life insurance agent.
    C. Life insurance is an ideal medium for funding a buy-sell agreement because, for a reasonable premium, it makes money available when needed to activate the sale of the business.
    D. In a sole proprietor buy-sell agreement, the sole proprietor is the owner of the policy.

8. Which of the following statements pertaining to partnership buy-sell plans is CORRECT?

    A. By law, a partnership ceases to exist when a partner dies.
    B. Homer and Wilbur are partners. Each buys an insurance policy to insure the life of the other; therefore, their buy-sell agreement is an entity plan.
    C. In a cross-purchase plan, the partnership is a party to the buy-sell agreement.
    D. A partnership buy-sell agreement can only work if there are only two partners involved.

9. Three equal partners in a business worth $600,000 decide to set up an insured cross-purchase buy-sell agreement. How large a policy would each partner buy to insure the lives of the other partners?

    A. $50,000
    B. $100,000
    C. $150,000
    D. $200,000

10. Hazel, Philip and Anita are equal partners in a partnership worth $150,000. They decide to arrange an insured cross-purchase buy-sell agreement. Which of the following statements pertaining to this arrangement is CORRECT?

    A. Hazel will purchase and maintain a $25,000 life insurance policy each on the lives of Philip and Anita.
    B. The partnership will purchase and maintain a $50,000 policy on each of the partner's lives.
    C. If Hazel dies, Philip and Anita will each have a partnership interest of $50,000.
    D. Each individual partner must purchase and maintain a $50,000 policy on each of the other partner's lives.

11. With three partners in a business, how many life insurance policies would be required to insure an entity buy-sell plan?

    A. Three
    B. Six
    C. Eight
    D. Nine

12. A company with five partners is considering a buy-sell plan. All of the following statements pertaining to buy-sell plans and this partnership are correct EXCEPT

    A. if they decide on an insured entity buy-sell agreement, it would be funded with a total of five life insurance policies
    B. if they use a cross-purchase plan, each partner would have to purchase four policies, or a total of 20 policies
    C. if the company installed an entity buy-sell agreement, the business would be a party to the agreement
    D. no benefits will accrue to the partnership from the buy-sell agreement until one of the partners dies

13. A company's total stock is valued at $480,000 and held in equal shares by four stockholder-employees who have finalized an insured stock-redemption agreement. How much life insurance must be purchased on the life of each of the four individuals to fund the buy-sell plan?

    A. $90,000
    B. $120,000
    C. $180,000
    D. $480,000

14. All of the following descriptions of buy-sell plans in close corporations are correct EXCEPT

    A. A close corporation that has four stockholder-employees plans to set up an insured buy-sell agreement. A stock redemption plan will require fewer policies than a cross-purchase plan.
    B. A corporation has an insured cross-purchase buy-sell plan agreed to by the corporate president and vice president, the two owners. The president and vice president own and pay the premiums for the life insurance policies in the plan.
    C. A corporation has a stock redemption plan for its officers, all stockholder-employees. The total stock is valued at $600,000 and held equally by the three officers. A $200,000 policy will be purchased by the corporation on each of its three officers.
    D. Like a partnership, a corporation ceases to exist after the death of one of its owners. It is not necessary to make an agreement to dispose of a deceased stockholder's interests.

15. Assume a dentist is insured in a business overhead expense policy that pays maximum monthly benefits of $3,000. The dentist became disabled and had covered expenses for the month totaling $1,500. Benefits payable would be

    A. $1,500
    B. $3,000
    C. $3,150
    D. $4,500

16. Which of the following statements pertaining to key-person life insurance is CORRECT?

    A. The insured key person controls the policy.
    B. The policy is a company-owned asset.
    C. At the death of the key person, proceeds are paid to his or her beneficiary.
    D. The owner of a company cannot be considered a key person.

17. All of the following statements pertaining to key-person life insurance are correct EXCEPT

    A. A key employee is any person whose contribution to the success of a business is essential.
    B. The ABC Company insured the life of its company president for $150,000. The ABC Company is the owner of the key-executive policy.
    C. The ABC Company purchased a $75,000 permanent life insurance policy on its general sales manager five years ago. This likely was reflected each year in the company's balance sheet as a loss.
    D. The ABC Company is the beneficiary of the key-person life insurance policies on its president and general sales manager.

18. Who drafts the buy-sell agreement for a sole proprietor?

    A. An attorney-at-law
    B. A person of the proprietor's choice
    C. An insurance consultant
    D. A certified public accountant

19. All of the following statements pertaining to business key person health insurance are correct EXCEPT

    A. premiums are tax deductible as a business expense
    B. benefits, when paid, are treated as taxable income
    C. these policies are used to indemnify a business in the case of a merger with another company
    D. proceeds from the policy may be used to buy out the interest of a partner or stockholder who becomes totally disabled

20. Which of the following statements pertaining to key-person life insurance is CORRECT?

    A. A company insures the life of its controller with a key-employee life insurance policy. The premiums are tax deductible, but if the controller dies, the policy proceeds would be taxable.
    B. A corporation has key-executive life insurance on its president and vice president. The policies show a current total cash value of $15,500, which may be used by the corporation for emergencies.
    C. The owner of key-person life insurance is the key person, and the beneficiary is the business organization.
    D. Key-person life insurance provides a death benefit for the key-person's family equal to the benefit for the business organization.

21. At a certain point in time, an employee will have a nonforfeitable right to the money contributed to a pension plan by the employer. This right is known as a

    A. proprietary interest
    B. vested interest
    C. contributory interest
    D. possessive interest

22. All of the following statements pertaining to qualified pension plans are correct EXCEPT

    A. the employer's contributions on the employees' behalf are tax deductible to the employer
    B. the employer's contributions are limited in amount by current tax law
    C. the employer's contributions become fixed liabilities for the employer
    D. the interest on the employer's contributions is included in the employee's gross income and is currently taxable

23. Robert and his employer agree on the purchase of a split-dollar life insurance policy. If it's a traditional plan, each year, the employer will contribute to the premium an amount equal to

    A. one-half of the premium
    B. the annual dividend
    C. the increase in the policy's cash value
    D. two-thirds of the premium

24. All of the following statements regarding nonqualified deferred compensation plans are correct EXCEPT

    A. a deferred compensation plan is an unsecured promise made by an employer to pay an employee part of his or her compensation in the future
    B. under a nonqualified deferred compensation plan, an employee can rely on guaranteed future benefits
    C. the employer receives no tax deduction for the amount of the compensation deferred until such amounts are actually distributed
    D. most deferred compensation plans are unfunded

25. Which of the following statements pertaining to salary continuation plans is CORRECT?

    A. Like a deferred compensation plan, a salary continuation plan is funded by the employee.
    B. Like a deferred compensation plan, a salary continuation plan is a salary reduction-type plan.
    C. A business may set up a salary continuation plan with an independent contractor.
    D. Like a deferred compensation plan, a salary continuation plan gives the employee benefits in lieu of a current raise or bonus.

26. Which of the following would be a source of instant liquidity upon the death of an estate owner?

    A. His or her home
    B. Debts payable to the estate
    C. A life insurance policy on the estate owner's life, payable to the estate
    D. Bank certificates of deposits

27. All of the following statements about how a life insurance policy could benefit a qualified charitable organization are correct EXCEPT

    A. the policy and its values could be assigned outright to the organization
    B. the organization could be named as the policy's beneficiary
    C. a death benefit used as a charitable gift can be contested by the insured's relatives
    D. life insurance proceeds are not part of the insured-donor's estate

28. John names the United Way as the beneficiary of his $250,000 life insurance policy. At John's death, who is responsible for the income taxes payable on the lump sum proceeds received by the charity?

    A. John's estate
    B. The United Way
    C. The tax liability is split evenly between John's estate and the United Way.
    D. There is no income tax payable on the death proceeds.

29. All of the following are advantages of life insurance as property EXCEPT

    A. the death proceeds create an instant estate
    B. the death proceeds payable to a beneficiary are protected from the insured's creditors
    C. the death proceeds are exempt from federal estate tax
    D. the policy's value is guaranteed

Answers & Rationale

1.   A.   The human life value concept is based on the fact that individuals who are financially responsible for the welfare of themselves and others, have a monetary value. This value is equal to the sum of the individual's future earnings, discounted at a reasonable rate of interest. By this formula, insurance can be tailor-made to meet specific objectives.
QID: 1055

2.   D.   The economic value of a person can be determined by discounting estimated future net earnings plus interest.
QID: 1056

3.   C.   The final expense fund is the amount of cash required at death to pay for a deceased breadwinner's last illness and funeral costs, outstanding debts, federal and state death taxes and any other unpaid taxes, legal fees, court costs, executor's fees and the like.
QID: 1057

4.   B.   When a covered worker dies, a surviving spouse with small children usually will be eligible for Social Security benefits. However, Social Security cannot (nor was it designed to) meet all of the needs of the family when the breadwinner dies.
QID: 1058

5.   B.   The blackout period refers to that period during which no Social Security benefits are payable to a surviving spouse. This period begins when the youngest child reaches age 16 and continues until the surviving parent retires.
QID: 1059

6.   D.   The dependency period refers to that period following the death of a breadwinner during which the children are living at home. The need for family income is greatest while the children are growing up.
QID: 1060

7.   C.   When a sole proprietor dies, the business can come to a sudden halt unless some arrangement has been made beforehand to continue the business. A buy-sell agreement funded by a life insurance policy purchased by an employee (or other party) on the life of the proprietor will transfer the business from the owner to the other party at an agreed-upon price. The agreement must be drafted by an attorney.
QID: 1061

8.   A.   As partnerships are dissolved automatically by the death of a partner, it is vital that a binding buy-sell agreement be established by the partners while they are living. In an entity plan, the insurance is owned by the partnership; in a cross-purchase plan, each partner owns insurance on the lives of the other partners.
QID: 1062

9.   B.   Each partner's share of the $600,000 business equals $200,000. Thus, if each partner were to purchase a $100,000 policy covering the lives of the other two, the benefits payable at the death of a partner—a total of $200,000—would enable the two survivors to purchase the deceased's interest in full and retain an equal partnership basis.
QID: 1063

10.   A.   In a cross-purchase buy-sell agreement, the partners individually agree to purchase a proportional interest of the deceased partner. In turn, the executor of the deceased's estate is directed to sell the interest to the surviving partners. The partnership itself is not a party to the agreement.
QID: 1064

11.   A.   In an entity agreement, the partnership acquires and maintains a life insurance policy on the lives of each partner. In contrast, in a cross-purchase buy-sell agreement, the partners individually agree to purchase the interest of the deceased partner. The number of life policies necessary to fund the agreement can be determined by the following formula, where n equals the number of partners $n \times (n - 1)$.
QID: 1065

12. D. A buy-sell plan offers several advantages to the partners while they all are living. Customers and employees feel comfortable about the future of the business because they know the death of a partner will not destroy the business. In addition, partners themselves have more peace of mind.
QID: 1066

13. B. The amount of insurance carried by the corporation on the lives of these stockholders is equal to each shareholder's proportionate share of the purchase price, or $120,000.
QID: 1067

14. D. In a close corporation, a buy-sell plan provides multiple advantages for all concerned. It usually takes one of two forms a cross-purchase plan in which the stockholders purchase the interest of the deceased stockholder as individuals and a stock redemption plan in which the corporation purchases the deceased stockholder's shares. In the case of multiple stockholders, a stock redemption plan requires fewer policies than a cross-purchase plan. A corporation does NOT cease to exist because an owner dies, and it is necessary to arrange for the disposition of the deceased owner's interests.
QID: 1068

15. A. Business overhead expense insurance reimburses businesses for actual overhead expenses in the event the business owner becomes disabled. In this case, the actual expenses totaled $1,500.
QID: 1069

16. B. A key person is any person in an organization whose contributions are essential to its success. With key-person insurance, the owner, premium-payer and beneficiary of the policy is the business. The purpose of the insurance is to protect the business against the economic loss incurred if the key person were to die.
QID: 1070

17. C. With key-person insurance, the business itself is the owner, premium-payer and beneficiary of the policy. As a result, the policy can be considered a company-owned asset, not a loss.
QID: 1071

18. A. It is important that the plan be drawn up as a legal document and be enforceable as such. Since only those duly licensed professionals may practice law, the agreement should be drafted by an attorney-at-law.
QID: 1072

19. C. Business health insurance is a form of key-person insurance used to indemnify a business for the loss of the services of a key employee or partner, or to buy out the interest of a partner or stockholder who has become totally disabled. As such, its cost is deductible as a business expense, and benefits payable are taxable income. It is not designed to address mergers.
QID: 1073

20. B. The death proceeds or cash values of key-person insurance are a company-controlled asset, available to the company to use for emergencies. Death proceeds from the policy are not taxable nor are premiums tax-deductible.
QID: 1074

21. B. After a specified number of years, an employee becomes 100 percent vested. That is, the employee has a nonforfeitable, ownership interest of 100 percent of the contributions made on his or her behalf.
QID: 1075

22. D. A qualified pension plan meets requirements set by the federal government in order to receive favorable tax treatment. This includes the deductibility of employer contributions, and the deferral of taxes on the amount of the contributions (and the income earned) for the employee. The employer's contributions, which are limited by law, are considered liabilities to the employer.
QID: 1076

23. C. Split-dollar insurance plans enable an employer and a select employee to share premium payments toward the purchase of insurance on the employee's life. Generally, the employer contributes to the premium each year an amount equal to the increase in the policy's cash value; the employee pays the balance. At death, the employer is entitled to receive from the proceeds an amount equal to its share of the premium payments (or the cash value, if greater); the employee's beneficiary receives the balance.
QID: 1077

24. B. Since most nonqualified deferred compensation plans are unfunded, an employee cannot rely on guaranteed future benefits. Typically, the employer finances its obligations on a pay-as-you-go basis.
QID: 1078

25. C. Salary continuation plans are established as a fringe benefit to continue an employee's salary (or a portion of it) after the employee retires or becomes disabled. The money to be paid is in addition to current salary and bonuses. Deferred compensation plans are agreements between employers and employees whereby the employee reduces his or her own income by deferring the receipt of currently due salary, bonus, commission or raise until a future date. In essence, a salary continuation plan is funded by the employer; a deferred compensation plan is funded by the employee. A salary continuation plan may be set up between an employer and employees or between a business and an independent contractor.
QID: 1079

26. C. Instant liquidity means property that is readily convertible into cash without loss, or cash itself. In this example, the only asset that would provide instant liquidity would be the life insurance policy.
QID: 1080

27. C. A life insurance policy can be gifted outright, meaning that the charitable organization becomes the owner of the policy's values. In this case, depending on how the donor and donee have set up the gift, the donor could continue to pay the premium or the charitable organization could take over the premium payments so the policy will pay its full benefit at the donor's death. As an alternative, a charitable organization could simply be named the beneficiary of the policy's proceeds, payable upon the insured's death.
QID: 1081

28. D. Lump-sum proceeds payable upon the death of the insured are not subject to income tax, regardless of the beneficiary.
QID: 1082

29. C. Life insurance proceeds can be subject to the federal estate tax if the proceeds are paid to the insured-owner's estate or if the insured-owner held any incidents of ownership in the policy.
QID: 1083

3

Insurance Industry Regulations

1. What did passage of the McCarran-Ferguson Act accomplish with respect to the regulation of the insurance industry?

   A. Assured continued state regulation of insurance
   B. Taxed insurance companies for additional federal revenue
   C. Deemed insurance a form of interstate commerce
   D. Exempted insurance from all federal government regulation and taxation

2. What is the purpose of the Fair Credit Reporting Act?

   A. It prohibits insurance companies from obtaining reports on applicants from outside investigative agencies.
   B. It gives consumers the right to question reports made about them by investigative agencies.
   C. It protects credit companies during the course of their investigations.
   D. It guarantees that credit reports will remain confidential and not accessible to businesses that do not sell insurance.

3. All of the following statements pertaining to the Fair Credit Reporting Act are correct EXCEPT

   A. a life insurance company obtains a consumer report on Burl, an applicant, without advising him of its intended action. The company has violated the Fair Credit Reporting Act.
   B. Peg has an application for life insurance rejected because of an unfavorable consumer report. She has a right to know what information the reporting agency has and can insist that any errors in the data be corrected.
   C. the Fair Credit Reporting Act is a state law that helps to assure accurate reporting of information about consumers.
   D. the Fair Credit Reporting Act does not apply to insurance companies who use their own staffs to investigate an applicant for insurance

4. Among their duties, state insurance departments are responsible for all of the following EXCEPT

   A. examining insurers' books and records
   B. defining and controlling the kinds of insurance contracts that may be sold
   C. investigating complaints of insureds
   D. creating the advertisements that the insurers use

5. All of the following are areas of operation in which state insurance departments are engaged EXCEPT

   A. Issuing rules and regulations to control the business of insurance
   B. Licensing insurers, agents and brokers
   C. Approving policy forms and rates
   D. Voting in state legislatures on insurance-related issues

6. The National Association of Insurance Commissioners (NAIC) has all of the following objectives EXCEPT

   A. to help protect policyowners' interests
   B. to assist with the formulation and passage of federal insurance legislation
   C. to encourage uniformity in state insurance laws and regulations
   D. to promote efficiency on the part of officials who administer insurance laws and regulations

7. Which of the following statements pertaining to the NAIC is CORRECT?

   A. It is a federal agency devoted to assisting states in regulating the insurance business.
   B. It is an association of top state insurance officials that has as one of its objectives, the uniformity of state insurance laws and regulations.
   C. It provides low-cost insurance to individuals who cannot purchase insurance through conventional channels.
   D. It administers the Medicaid program in each state.

8. All of the following must have a license in order to sell insurance EXCEPT a(n)

   A. insurer
   B. agent
   C. broker
   D. client service representative employed by an insurer

9. In most jurisdictions, all of the following would constitute unlawful acts of rebating EXCEPT

   A. sharing a sales commission with a policyowner
   B. sending a new policyowner on an expense-paid trip to Florida
   C. sending holiday greeting cards to policyowners
   D. reducing the initial premium payable on an insurance policy

10. Which of the following is considered rebating?

    A. Leading someone to believe that coverage exists when, in fact, it does not exist
    B. Commission splitting between agents
    C. Offering a client anything of value for purchasing insurance
    D. Persuading a client to drop an existing insurance policy to purchase another

11. All of the following statements pertaining to violations of ethical selling are correct EXCEPT

    A. in some states, both the agent and a policyowner who are found guilty of rebating would be subject to penalties
    B. rebating is unlawful largely because it is a form of discrimination.
    C. if an agent is convicted in a case of twisting, it can be said that he or she is probably guilty of rebating
    D. only when it is in the best interest of the policyowner should a policy replacement be recommended

12. Assume an agent stresses the following points in a sales interview while recommending a participating 30-pay life policy to a 37-year-old prospect. Which statement constitutes misrepresentation?

    A. The policy's cash value will build at a faster rate than in a straight life policy.
    B. The policy will be fully paid up in 30 years.
    C. The policy endows in 30 years.
    D. Dividends are not guaranteed for the future.

13. Twisting may involve any of the following actions on the part of a life insurance agent EXCEPT

    A. misrepresenting the terms of a proposed policy to a prospect
    B. making an incomplete comparison of two different policies
    C. misrepresenting the provisions of a policyowner's existing policy to promote the sale of another policy
    D. converting a client's convertible term policy to permanent insurance

14. Misrepresentation is

    A. leading someone to believe that an insurance policy provides certain benefits when it does not do so
    B. encouraging policyowners to drop existing insurance for another similar policy
    C. offering an inducement for the purchase of insurance
    D. suggesting that a client replace term insurance with whole life

15. All of the following violate ethical principles in the selling of insurance EXCEPT

    A. rebating
    B. misrepresentation
    C. replacement
    D. twisting

16. Which of the following statements regarding policy replacement is CORRECT?

    A. Policy replacement is prohibited by law in all states.
    B. Twisting and replacement are synonymous terms.
    C. Even if the customer wants to replace his or her existing policy, agents can effect a policy replacement only by following the replacement regulations in their state.
    D. Premiums for replacement policies are generally lower than for the existing policies they replace.

17. All of the following statements pertaining to an agent's handling of premium money are correct EXCEPT

    A. An agent must not make personal use of premium money received from policyowners.
    B. An agent violating regulations concerning handling premium money may be charged with embezzlement or mishandling funds.
    C. An agent holds premium money for the insured.
    D. An agent may spend premium money for his or her own personal use.

18. All of the following statements pertaining to unethical selling are correct EXCEPT

    A. An agent tells a prospect that future policy dividends will be as much or more as are being paid currently. The agent is guilty of misrepresentation.
    B. An agent asserts to an applicant that the incontestable clause in a policy means that the policy can never be contested. The agent is guilty of misrepresentation.
    C. An agent states to a prospect that a competing insurer is charging lower premiums because it is hurting for business. The agent is guilty of defamation.
    D. An agent knowingly submits an application that contains false information. The agent is guilty of twisting.

19. The origin of the Unfair Trade Practices Act is

    A. federal law
    B. state law
    C. NAIC model legislation
    D. SEC directive

20. The result of the Unfair Trade Practices Act was to empower state insurance departments with all of the following authority EXCEPT

    A. investigating false financial statements
    B. issuing cease and desist orders
    C. imposing penalties
    D. licensing insurers and producers

21. Which of the following legislation requires fair and accurate reporting of a consumer's buying and bill-paying history?

    A. Unfair Trade Practices Act
    B. McCarran-Ferguson Act
    C. Employee Retirement Income Security Act
    D. Fair Credit Reporting Act

22. What did the Financial Services Modernization Act accomplish with respect to the regulation of the insurance industry?

    A. Barred common ownership of banks and insurance companies
    B. Ensured continued state regulation of insurance
    C. Permitted banks, securities firms and insurance companies to enter each other's lines of business
    D. Exempted the insurance industry from federal government regulation

23. All of the following statements about life insurance policy replacement are correct EXCEPT

    A. Replacement transactions generally are illegal.
    B. The agent must explain why a policy is being replaced in the application form.
    C. The agent must be able to demonstrate that policy replacement is a suitable recommendation.
    D. The existing insurer and the replacing insurer must be notified of the intended replacement.

24. Which of the following statements regarding an agent's ethical duties is NOT correct?

    A. The agent must determine the client's needs.
    B. The agent must determine whether the recommended insurance product is in the client's best interest.
    C. The agent should disclose both the limitations and benefits of an insurance product.
    D. The agent's relationship with the client generally ends when a sale is completed.

25. Which of the following statements about state guaranty associations is CORRECT?

    A. Each state funds its own association.
    B. They cover consumers' unpaid claims if an insurer becomes insolvent.
    C. They only help impaired but not insolvent insurers.
    D. They have been established in most states.

Answers & Rationale

1.   A.   The McCarran-Ferguson Act allowed the regulation of insurance to remain in the hands of the states as long as they did an effective job. States were encouraged to improve and make more uniform their regulation of the insurance industry.
QID: 1084

2.   B.   The Fair Credit Reporting Act is a federal law that helps assure confidential, fair and accurate reporting of information about consumers, including applicants for insurance. It does not preclude insurance companies from obtaining outside reports; however, it allows consumers to request disclosure of information contained in their reports.
QID: 1085

3.   C.   The Fair Credit Reporting Act is a federal law, not a state law. As corrected, the statement is also true.
QID: 1086

4.   D.   State insurance departments are involved in virtually every phase of the insurance process. This includes examining insurers' books and records, defining, monitoring and controlling the kinds of contracts sold, investigating insureds' complaints, issuing rules and regulations, licensing insurers, agents and brokers, and approving policy forms and rates.
QID: 1087

5.   D.   State insurance departments are involved in virtually every phase of the insurance process. This includes examining insurers' books and records, defining, monitoring and controlling the kinds of contracts sold, investigating insureds' complaints, issuing rules and regulations, licensing insurers, agents and brokers, and approving policy forms and rates.
QID: 1088

6.   B.   The NAIC is an association of state insurance commissioners, directors and superintendents. It has nothing to do with the federal government. In fact, it seeks to preserve the continued regulation of insurance by the states.
QID: 1089

7.   B.   The NAIC is an association of state insurance commissioners, directors and superintendents. It has nothing to do with the federal government. In fact, it seeks to preserve the continued regulation of insurance by the states.
QID: 1090

8.   D.   Insurers and producers (agents and brokers) selling insurance in a given state must be licensed in that state for that purpose.
QID: 1091

9.   C.   Rebating requires an agent to give an insured something of value, such as part of the agent's commission or a substantial gift. Sending greeting cards is a simple marketing gesture of goodwill.
QID: 1092

10.   C.   Rebating is offering a client anything of value for purchasing the insurance.
QID: 1093

11.   C.   If an agent is guilty of twisting (making incomplete or untrue comparisons to coerce a sale), he or she may not be guilty of rebating (an illegal offering of something of value, such as a return of premiums to induce a sale).
QID: 1094

12.   C.   Any written or oral statement that does not tell the truth about a policy is a misrepresentation. A 30-pay life policy does not endow (reach a point at which cash value equals face amount) in 30 years; it is simply paid up.
QID: 1095

13. D. Twisting involves misrepresentations and incomplete comparisons with the intention of coercing a sale. It does not involve the normal servicing of a client's account, such as converting a term policy to permanent insurance.
QID: 1096

14. A. Misrepresentation is any false or misleading statement made with respect to an insurance policy. An example of misrepresentation is leading someone to believe that an insurance policy provides certain benefits when, in fact, it does not.
QID: 1097

15. C. Replacement, a legal practice, involves replacing one policy with the purchase of another. When replacement occurs, it must adhere to existing state regulations involving full and fair disclosure.
QID: 1098

16. C. State laws do not prevent a policyowner from replacing one insurance policy with another, as long as the transaction is handled in accordance with state laws and procedures.
QID: 1099

17. D. An agent enjoys a fiduciary role with an insured. This establishes a relationship of trust. As a result, the agent must be very careful in handling money received from the insured and the company's premiums or be subject to harsh penalties.
QID: 1100

18. D. If an agent makes any written or oral statement that does not tell the exact and full truth about a policy's terms or benefits or if he or she defames another company, the agent is guilty of misrepresentation and defamation, which violate ethical sales practices.
QID: 1101

19. C. The Unfair Trade Practices Act is a piece of NAIC model legislation adopted by most states, giving state insurance departments the power to investigate and control the business practices of insurers and producers.
QID: 1102

20. D. The Unfair Trade Practices Act, a piece of NAIC model legislation adopted by most states, gives insurance commissioners the power to investigate alleged improper insurance practices—such as improper finances, false financial statements, boycotts or coercion—and issue cease and desist orders and penalties if necessary.
QID: 1103

21. D. The Fair Credit Reporting Act protects an individual's privacy during the course of a credit check. If any consumer report is used to deny insurance coverage or charge higher rates, the insurer must furnish to the applicant the name of the reporting agency conducting the investigation. Any insurance company that fails to do so is liable to the consumer for actual and punitive damages.
QID: 1104

22. C. The Financial Services Modernization Act repealed the Glass-Steagall Act, which barred common ownership of banks, insurance companies and securities firms and erected a wall of separation between banks and nonfinancial companies. Under the FSMA, commercial banks, investment banks, retail brokerages and insurance companies can enter each other's lines of business.
QID: 3300

23. A. The practice of replacement, which involves convincing a policyowner to lapse or terminate an existing policy and replace it with another, is not illegal. However, because replacement could pose serious financial consequences for the policyowner, the agent must follow certain policy replacement guidelines that protect the policyowner. For example, the agent must demonstrate that policy replacement is a suitable recommendation and must explain why a policy is being

replaced in the application form. The agent must also notify both the existing and replacing insurer of the intended replacement.
QID: 3301

24.   D.   The ethical agent determines what needs the client has and then determines the product best suited to meet those needs. The agent should also fully inform clients about all aspects of the recommended products—their limitations as well as their benefits. After a sale is completed, however, the agent's relationship with the client does not end. Routine follow-up calls are recommended, for example, to ensure that the client's needs are always covered.
QID: 3302

25.   B.   All states have established guaranty funds or associations. If an insurer becomes financially unable to pay its claims, the state guaranty association will cover the consumers' unpaid claims. Insurance companies fund state guaranty associations through assessments.
QID: 3303

Legal Principles of the Insurance Contract

1. An insurance contract is prepared by one party, the insurer, rather than by negotiation between the contracting parties. Which of the following statements explains this characteristic of insurance?

   A. The insurance contract is an aleatory contract.
   B. The insurance contract is a conditional contract.
   C. The insurance contract is a contract of adhesion.
   D. The insurance contract is a unilateral contract.

2. Parties to an insurance contract must act in "utmost good faith," which means both agent and applicant

   A. make no attempt to deceive each other
   B. work together to find insurance for the lowest possible price
   C. always arrive on time for meetings
   D. agree to transact insurance business

3. With regard to insurance, the term "consideration" means the

   A. price of the contract (the premium)
   B. insurer's method of evaluating the applicant for coverage
   C. screening process all agents undergo prior to licensing
   D. side-by-side policy comparison by the applicant

4. A contract is voidable when it

   A. lacks one of the basic elements of a legal contract
   B. is binding unless the party with the right to set it aside wishes to do so
   C. was never in effect
   D. cannot be enforced by either party

5. Who are the parties to a life insurance contract?

   A. Agent and the applicant
   B. Agent, the applicant and the beneficiary
   C. Applicant and the beneficiary
   D. Applicant and the insuring company

6. "The applicant for insurance has more to gain if the insured continues to live than if the insured dies" is the rule defining

   A. one's legal capacity to enter into an insurance contract
   B. insurable interest
   C. a legal wagering contract
   D. the aleatory nature of an insurance contract

7. Alan, age 39, is married and has one small son. He is employed as a sales manager by R.J. Links, a sole proprietorship that owes much of its success to Alan's efforts. He recently borrowed $50,000 from his brother-in-law, Pete, to finance a vacation home. Based on these facts, which of the following do(es) NOT have an insurable interest in Alan's life?

   A. His spouse
   B. His employer
   C. His brother-in-law
   D. His customers

8. In legal terms, voluntary relinquishment of a known right is called a

   A. waiver
   B. concealment
   C. warranty
   D. withdrawal

9. With a life insurance contract, which of the contracting parties makes an enforceable promise?

   A. Insurer
   B. Applicant or owner
   C. Agent
   D. Beneficiary

10. Statements guaranteed to be true are called

    A. waivers
    B. estoppels
    C. warranties
    D. representations

11. All statements made by an applicant in an application for life insurance generally are considered to be

    A. warranties
    B. affirmations
    C. representations
    D. declarations

12. The intentional failure to disclose known facts on an insurance application is called

    A. concealment
    B. adhesion
    C. twisting
    D. misrepresentation

13. A false statement of fact is known as

    A. concealment
    B. adhesion
    C. aleatory
    D. misrepresentation

14. Since only the insurer prepares the insurance contract, it is called a contract of

    A. estoppel
    B. adhesion
    C. unilateral terms
    D. condition

15. The fact that an insurance contract promises to pay benefits contingent on a future uncertainty (such as death or illness) makes it what type of contract?

    A. Estoppel
    B. Adhesion
    C. Aleatory
    D. Conditional

16. Since the obligations of the insurance company hinge on certain acts of the policyowner, the beneficiary, or both, the insurance contract is termed

    A. bilateral
    B. unilateral
    C. aleatory
    D. conditional

17. Which of the following statements pertaining to a life insurance contract is CORRECT?

    A. The term "unilateral" refers to the legal obligations of the policyowner.
    B. The term "adhesion" indicates that a life insurance contract involves no exchange of equivalent values.
    C. The term "conditional" indicates that the insurer will pay benefits regardless of a loss.
    D. A "valued" contract pays a stated sum when the loss occurs.

18. Life insurance is all of the following EXCEPT a

    A. reimbursement-type contract
    B. valued contract
    C. unilateral contract
    D. legal contract

19. With a life insurance contract, an insurable interest must exist

    A. at the inception of the contract
    B. as long as the insured lives
    C. at the insured's death
    D. when the proceeds are paid out

20. An agent's primary responsibility is to

    A. collect premiums on a regular basis
    B. act in accordance with the agency agreement
    C. submit all applications promptly
    D. renew his or her license at the appropriate time

21. In carrying out their duties, licensed insurance agents are representatives of the

    A. insureds
    B. general public
    C. insurance company
    D. state insurance department

22. An insurance agent should be all of the following EXCEPT

    A. honest and trustworthy
    B. qualified to perform insurance functions
    C. reputable in business
    D. a college graduate

23. What kind of policy will protect an insurance agent against liability arising out of acts committed in his or her professional capacity?

    A. Indemnity
    B. Errors and omissions
    C. General liability
    D. Contractual liability

24. All of the following statements about life insurance are correct EXCEPT

    A. Life insurance is not a personal contract between the insurer and insured.
    B. A policyowner must notify the beneficiary before transferring ownership.
    C. A policyowner must notify the insurance company in writing to transfer a policy.
    D. If a policy is transferred, the new owner receives all of the rights of policyownership.

25. Which of the following statements about competent parties and life insurance contracts is NOT correct?

    A. Beneficiaries and insureds, if different from the applicant, do not have to be competent parties.
    B. Trusts and estates are considered competent parties that may enter into insurance contracts.
    C. Insurers are considered competent if they are licensed or authorized by the state in which they conduct business.
    D. Minors are not considered competent parties and can void an insurance contract at their option.

26. When an insurer accepts an agent's actions, even though they were beyond the scope of his or her authority, this is known as

    A. acquiescence
    B. ratification
    C. apparent authority
    D. implied authority

27. John's insurance contract states that it will pay $500,000 at his death. This type of a contract is known as a(n)

    A. indemnity contract
    B. conditional contract
    C. valued contract
    D. aleatory contract

28. After Joe died, ABC Insurer discovered that he had misrepresented his health status when he applied for a life insurance policy seven years ago. Which of the following statements about ABC Insurer is CORRECT?

    A. It can void the policy.
    B. It does not have to pay the death benefit.
    C. It must prove the misrepresentation was material before voiding the policy.
    D. It cannot void or revoke the policy.

29. Which of the following statements describes the parole evidence rule?

    A. A written contract cannot be changed once it is signed.
    B. An oral contract generally cannot be modified by oral evidence.
    C. A written contract generally cannot be changed by oral evidence.
    D. An oral contract takes precedence over any earlier written contracts.

30. Which of the following terms indicates that a life insurance contract contains the enforceable promises of only one party?

    A. Adhesion
    B. Unilateral
    C. Conditional
    D. Aleatory

31. With regard to life insurance, all of the following statements are correct EXCEPT

    A. individuals are considered to have insurable interests in themselves
    B. spouses have insurable interests in each other
    C. a partnership has an insurable interest in a partner
    D. an insurable interest must exist at the time of the claim

32. Stan and Gwen enter into a contract in which Stan agrees to fraudulently induce sick people to sell their insurance contracts to Gwen's company. Stan and Gwen's contract can best be described as

    A. void
    B. competitive
    C. voidable
    D. conditional

Answers & Rationale

1.   C.   Insurance contracts are contracts of adhesion, meaning that they are prepared by one party, the insurer. They are not negotiated contracts. In effect, the applicant "adheres" to the terms of the contract when he or she accepts it.
QID: 1105

2.   A.   Both the policyowner and the insurer must know all material facts and relevant information. There can be no attempt by either party to conceal, disguise or deceive. A consumer purchases a policy based largely on what the insurer and its agent claim are its features, benefits and advantages. An insurer issues a policy based primarily on what the applicant reveals in the application.
QID: 1106

3.   A.   Legally defined, "consideration" is the price requested and given in exchange for a promise or an act. In terms of insurance, it is the price of the contract, or the premium, the insured pays to keep the contract and its promised benefits in force.
QID: 1107

4.   B.   A voidable contract is an agreement which, for a reason satisfactory to a court, may be set aside by one of the parties to the contract. Unless and until the contract is disaffirmed by one of its parties, however, it remains enforceable.
QID: 1108

5.   D.   The parties to a life insurance contract are the applicant and the insuring company. Neither the beneficiary nor the agent is a contracting party.
QID: 1109

6.   B.   A person acquiring a life insurance contract must be subject to loss upon the death of the individual to be insured. This is known as insurable interest and it is required before a life insurance policy will be issued.
QID: 1110

7.   D.   Generally, a person has an insurable interest in another if they are related by blood or marriage or if their relationship is such that the insured's continuing to live will benefit that individual or the insured's death will cause that individual financial or economic loss. Spouses are assumed to have an automatic insurable interest in each other. Thus, in this case, all three individuals have an insurable interest in Alan's life.
QID: 1111

8.   A.   A waiver is a voluntary relinquishment of a known right. If an insurer waives a legal right under an insurance policy, it cannot deny a future claim based on a violation of that right. This is known as estoppel, and the insurer is "estopped" from denying the claim.
QID: 1112

9.   A.   A life insurance contract is unilateral in that only one party—the insurer—makes an enforceable promise (the promise to pay the policy's benefit if certain occurrences come to pass or certain conditions are met). The applicant or owner makes no enforceable promise and is not legally required to maintain the contract (by continuing to pay the premiums.) The owner can let the policy lapse at any time. Of course, once the owner stops paying the premiums, the insurer can cancel the policy.
QID: 1113

10.   C.   Warranties are statements guaranteed to be true. Representations are statements believed to be true.
QID: 1114

11.   C.   Most states have passed statutes specifying that, except in instances of fraud, all statements made by an applicant when applying for insurance are considered to be representations.
QID: 1115

12. A. If the applicant intentionally fails to disclose known facts that could influence the issuance of the policy (concealment), the insurer may have the grounds for voiding the policy.
QID: 1116

13. D. False statements of facts, known as misrepresentations, may provide grounds for voiding the policy, even if unintentional.
QID: 1117

14. B. Insurance contracts are contracts of adhesion, meaning that they are prepared by one party, the insurer. They are not negotiated contracts. In effect, the applicant adheres to the terms of the contract when he or she accepts it.
QID: 1118

15. C. Insurance is an aleatory contract in that the benefit it pays is contingent upon the occurrence of a future uncertain event, such as illness or death. An aleatory contract is defined as "a mutual agreement in which the effects, in respect to both losses and advantages, depend on an uncertain event."
QID: 1119

16. D. Insurance is a conditional contract because the obligations of the insurance company hinge on the performance of certain acts by the owner and the beneficiary, such as the payment of premiums and furnishing proof of loss.
QID: 1120

17. D. A "unilateral contract" in insurance refers to the insurer's legal obligations. "Adhesion" indicates that the contract was drafted by one party (the insurer) and must be accepted or rejected by a second party (the applicant), who cannot bargain with respect to its terms. "Conditional" refers to the fact that the insurer's promise to pay benefits is conditioned on the occurrence of a loss. A "valued" contract pays a stated sum, regardless of the value of the actual loss.
QID: 1121

18. A. Life insurance is a valued contract in that it pays a stated amount. Health insurance is a reimbursement contract, reimbursing the insured for the amount of loss.
QID: 1122

19. A. With life insurance, an insurable interest is only required upon policy application and inception. It does not have to continue through the duration of the contract, nor does it have to exist at the insured's death in order to claim the policy's proceeds. This is in contrast to property and casualty insurance, which requires that an insurable interest exist at the time of the claim.
QID: 1123

20. B. The agency agreement is the agent's contract with the insurance company. It defines the conditions under which the agent agrees to represent the company and governs the agent's activities on behalf of the company.
QID: 1124

21. C. An agent is a person or corporation authorized by an insurer to solicit business and collect money on behalf of the insurer.
QID: 1125

22. D. An insurance agent must be honest, trustworthy, qualified and have a good business reputation.
QID: 1126

23. B. Under errors and omissions insurance (E & O), the insurer agrees to pay for claims arising out of the errors and omissions of the insured agent. It is a professional liability insurance policy.
QID: 1127

24. B. Life insurance is not a personal contract between the insurer and the insured. Policyowners actually own their policies and can give them away if they wish. To transfer a policy, a policyowner must simply notify the company in writing. It does not need to notify the beneficiary. The new owner is then granted all of the rights of policyownership.
QID: 3305

25. D. To be enforceable, an insurance contract must be entered into by competent parties. An insurer is considered competent if licensed or authorized by the state in which it conducts business. Because beneficiaries and insureds (if different from the applicant) are not parties to the contract, they do not have to have contractual capability. Trusts and estates are also competent parties and in some states, minors of a certain age have the capacity to enter into valid and enforceable life insurance contracts. In the absence of such a statute, insurance contracts with minors are voidable at the minor's option.
QID: 3306

26. B. Even if an agent does not have the express or implied authority to take a particular action, his or her authority may be extended by ratification. Ratification occurs when the insurer accepts the agent's actions that were beyond the scope of his or her authority and acts as if the agent actually had authority to take such actions.
QID: 3307

27. C. John's insurance contract is a valued contract. It pays a stated sum, regardless of the actual loss incurred, when the contingency insured against occurs. Because John acquired a life insurance policy insuring his life for $500,000, that is the amount payable at death. There is no attempt to value "actual" financial loss. An indemnity contract, on the other hand, pays an amount equal to the loss—it attempts to return the insured to his or her original financial position.
QID: 3308

28. D. In most cases, life insurers have only a limited period of time to uncover false warranties, misrepresentations or concealment. After that time period passes, usually two years from policy issue, the contract cannot be voided or revoked for these reasons.
QID: 3309

29. C. The parole evidence rule states that when parties put their agreement in writing, all previous verbal statements come together in that writing, and a written contract cannot be changed or modified by parole (oral) evidence. There are a few exceptions, however. For example, parole evidence may be admissible when the written contract terms are incomplete or ambiguous.
QID: 3310

30. B. Insurance contracts are unilateral in that only one party—the insurer—makes any kind of enforceable promise. Insurers promise to pay benefits when a certain event occurs, such as death or disability. The applicant makes no such promise—he or she does not even promise to pay premiums, and the insurer cannot require that they be paid. In contrast, with a bilateral contract, each contracting party makes enforceable promises.
QID: 3311

31. D. In a valid insurance contract, the applicant must have an insurable interest in the insured, which means that the applicant must be subject to loss if the insured dies. Many relationships such as husband and wife and partner and partnership provide the basis for an insurable interest. An insurable interest is required only when a contract is issued. It does not have to be maintained throughout the life of the contract, nor is it necessary at the time of claim.
QID: 3312

32. A. Stan and Gwen's contract would be considered a void contract because it lacks one of the elements specified by law for a valid contract. In this case the contract has an illegal purpose (fraudulently inducing sick individuals to sell their insurance policies) and neither party to the contract can enforce it.
QID: 3313

Part Two

Principles of Life Insurance

5

Types of Life Insurance Policies and Riders

1. Jason is the insured in a $100,000, ten-year renewable term policy. Soon after taking out the policy, he develops a serious heart condition. Which of the following statements pertaining to Jason's rights to renew this policy is CORRECT?

   A. Since the condition manifested after the policy was issued, he will not be able to renew his policy.
   B. Jason will be able to renew the policy.
   C. It will be necessary for Jason to show evidence of insurability in order to renew the policy.
   D. If Jason renews his policy, it will be rated for his health condition.

2. Which of the following statements about a one-year renewable term policy is CORRECT?

   A. Its premium increases each year, based on the insured's health.
   B. It has a premium that remains the same, no matter how many times it is renewed.
   C. It renews with an increase in premium, based on the insured's age.
   D. It may not be renewed more than once.

3. David has a $300,000 nonrenewable five-year term policy. The premium he pays for this policy would be

   A. more than for a $300,000, five-year renewable term policy
   B. the same as for a $300,000, five-year renewable term policy
   C. less than for a $300,000, five-year renewable term policy
   D. increased each year during the five-year period

4. Madge took out a $100,000, ten-year convertible term policy at age 30 and at age 36 decides to convert the policy to permanent insurance of the same amount on an original-age basis. All of the following statements pertaining to this situation are correct EXCEPT

   A. Conversion will be contingent upon her evidence of insurability.
   B. The new policy will build cash values at a faster rate than if she converts at her attained age.
   C. A higher premium will be charged for the new policy.
   D. She must make up the difference in premiums for the period between her ages 30 and 36.

5. Which of the following statements pertaining to term insurance is CORRECT?

   A. A term policy cannot be both renewable and convertible.
   B. Janice and Ruth are the same age and have term policies of identical face amounts. Janice's policy is renewable; Ruth's policy is nonrenewable. Ruth pays the higher premium.
   C. Bob decides to exercise an option to renew his term insurance, but first he must pass a physical examination.
   D. Term insurance provides protection for only a temporary period of time.

6. Which of the following life insurance policies having the same face value would have the highest premium if issued to the same person?

   A. Ten-year renewable level term
   B. Ten-year renewable and convertible level term
   C. Ten-year decreasing term
   D. Ten-year nonrenewable level term

7. Gerald, a 40-year-old building contractor, wants financial protection for his family while $150,000 of his assets are tied up in a building project for about five years. Which of the following types of life insurance policies would give him that protection at the lowest cost?

   A. Straight whole life
   B. Life paid-up at 45
   C. 5-year level term
   D. Single-premium whole life

8. Avis has a term insurance policy in which the amount of protection remains constant during the term period. Which kind of term insurance does Avis have?

   A. Family term
   B. Increasing term
   C. Decreasing term
   D. Level term

9. Peggy takes out a $50,000 ten-year policy on herself and names her two children, ages 11 and 12, as primary beneficiaries to share equally in the proceeds. How much would each child receive if Peggy should die when the children are ages 19 and 20, respectively?

   A. Nothing
   B. $25,000
   C. $50,000
   D. $50,000 plus the cash value in the policy

10. Frank is the insured in a $40,000, five-year level term policy issued in 1994. He died in 2000. His beneficiary received

    A. the cash value of the policy
    B. $20,000
    C. $40,000
    D. nothing

11. Chester, age 25, has a $25,000, 15-year level term policy. Joel has a $25,000, 15-year decreasing term contract. The policies were issued by the same company to the respective insureds on September 1, 1984. Which of the following statements pertaining to this situation is CORRECT?

    A. Chester and Joel had the same amount of protection during the 15-year periods of their policies.
    B. If both insureds had died in 1998, Chester's beneficiary would have received more than Joel's beneficiary.
    C. Chester and Joel pay the same amount of premium.
    D. If both insureds had died in 2000, Chester's beneficiary would have received less than Joel's beneficiary.

12. Decreasing term insurance could be recommended for all of the following EXCEPT

    A. to protect a family while children are growing up
    B. for mortgage protection
    C. for protection while a business loan is outstanding
    D. to build a retirement fund

13. Roland is 45 years old and married. He has a son who is age 19 and a freshman at a local university. He also has a daughter, age eight. A decreasing term policy could be recommended for Roland for which of the following reasons?

    A. To supplement Roland's retirement income
    B. To guarantee that his son's college tuition will be covered
    C. To provide (an emergency) source for loans
    D. To provide a future college education for the daughter

14. Increasing term insurance is almost always sold as a(an)

    A. option
    B. rider
    C. endorsement
    D. whole life policy

15. In most states, credit life insurance is sold in the form of

    A. whole life
    B. increasing term
    C. decreasing term
    D. level term

16. The party to whom the life insurance policy cash values belong is the

    A. policyowner
    B. insured
    C. insurer
    D. beneficiary

17. How can the cash value accumulation in a straight whole life insurance policy be accessed while the insured is living and while keeping the coverage in force?

    A. Through a policy loan
    B. Through a cash value surrender
    C. Through a partial cash value withdrawal
    D. Through a dividend payment

18. A life insurance policy in which the face amount remains level and the cash value grows to an amount equal to the face amount when the insured reaches age 100 is a(n)

    A. whole life policy
    B. decreasing term policy
    C. endowment policy
    D. level term

19. All of the following statements pertaining to a whole life policy are correct EXCEPT

    A. The policy offers insurance protection to age 100.
    B. It provides both insurance protection and "living" values.
    C. It is designed to mature or endow at the insured's age 100.
    D. The face amount may be paid as a lump sum at the policyowner's selected retirement age.

20. All of the following are distinguishing characteristics of straight whole life policies EXCEPT

    A. insurance protection to age 100
    B. cash values
    C. level premiums
    D. option to renew

21. Darlene owned a $100,000 whole life policy that had a $75,000 cash value when she died at the age of 75. The amount paid by the insurance company as a death benefit was

    A. nothing
    B. $75,000
    C. $100,000
    D. $175,000

22. Which of the following policies endows at age 100?

    A. Level term and whole life
    B. Whole life and limited pay life
    C. Endowment and decreasing term
    D. Any endowment policy

23. Tom has a $50,000 whole life policy. If he continued to pay the required premiums and lived to age 100, he would receive

    A. nothing, as he outlived the term of the contract
    B. $50,000 as an endowment
    C. the cash surrender value, a sum less than $50,000
    D. double the face amount, or $100,000

24. Which of the following statements pertaining to limited pay life policies is CORRECT?

    A. The total premium cost for a single-premium life policy is more than the total premium cost for a policy with premiums spread over a period of years.
    B. Both limited pay life and whole life policies endow at age 100.
    C. A limited pay life policyowner pays premium of variable amounts during the life of the policy.
    D. Insurance protection exists only during the time premiums are actually paid.

25. Which of the following $50,000 limited pay life policies will have the highest premium for an applicant who is age 30?

    A. 20-pay life policy
    B. 25-pay life policy
    C. 30-pay life policy
    D. Life paid-up at age 65

26. All of the following statements regarding basic forms of whole life insurance are correct EXCEPT

    A. Generally, straight life premiums are payable, at least annually, for the duration of the insured's life.
    B. The owner of a 30-pay life policy will owe no more premiums after the thirtieth year the policy is in force.
    C. Limited payment life provides protection only for the years during which premiums are paid.
    D. A single-premium life policy is purchased with a large one-time only premium.

27. Alan is the insured in a $50,000 endowment at age 60 policy he purchased in 1979 at the age of 40. How long did he pay premiums before the policy endowed?

    A. 20 years
    B. 40 years
    C. 60 years
    D. 100 years

28. At age 35, Brett bought a $25,000 life insurance policy for which the beneficiary will be paid the face amount if Brett dies before age 60. Brett is to pay the premiums until he reaches age 55, but the insurance protection continues to maturity. Which type of policy did Brett purchase?

    A. 20-pay endowment at age 60
    B. 20-pay life
    C. 30-year endowment
    D. Life paid-up at 65

29. How long does the insurance protection (amount at risk) extend in a 30-year endowment policy?

    A. To the insured's age 100
    B. 100 years
    C. To the insured's age 65
    D. 30 years

30. Which term would identify a policy in which the premium payments are paid for 20 years before the policy endows, at which time the insured turns age 60?

    A. Endowment at age 60 policy
    B. 20-pay life policy
    C. Whole life policy
    D. 20-pay endowment at age 60 policy

31. All of the following statements pertaining to a modified whole life policy are correct EXCEPT

    A. cash value builds up to the insured's age of 100 so long as the policy is in force
    B. premiums are uniformly lower during the early years of the contract
    C. it is basically an endowment policy
    D. the premium-paying period continues to age 100

32. Helen has just taken out a modified whole life policy. Which of the following statements pertaining to her policy is CORRECT?

    A. The premium will be higher during the next few years and then remain constant at a lower level.
    B. The premium will be lower during the next few years and then be increased to a higher constant level.
    C. The face amount will be higher during the next few years and then remain constant at a lower level.
    D. The face amount will be lower during the next few years and then be increased to a higher constant level.

33. Gene, age 20, purchased a $50,000 life insurance policy. The premium at issue is lower than normal whole life rates, and increases each year for the first five years of the policy period. After that, the premium levels off. What type of policy does Gene own?

    A. Modified whole life
    B. Minimum deposit whole life
    C. Graded premium whole life
    D. Limited pay at age 20 whole life

34. All of the following statements pertaining to modified whole life and graded premium whole life policies are correct EXCEPT

    A. the premium for modified whole life increases each year after the first few years of policy issue
    B. the premium for graded premium whole life increases each year during the first few years after policy issue
    C. modified whole life contracts build cash values and have premium-paying periods to age 100
    D. graded premium whole life policies build cash values and have premium-paying periods to age 100

35. A form of whole life insurance in which the face amount automatically increases as the Consumer Price Index increases is called

    A. modified whole life
    B. graded premium whole life
    C. indexed whole life
    D. term insurance

36. A life insurance policy under which the amount a policyowner pays in during the first years exceeds the sum of net level premiums that would have been payable to provide paid-up future benefits in seven years is called a(n)

    A. paid-up contract
    B. flexible premium contract
    C. modified endowment contract
    D. variable contract

37. All of the following statements pertaining to a 20-year family term insurance policy are correct EXCEPT

    A. it usually is sold in units, each valued at ten dollars or more
    B. it is a policy of decreasing term insurance
    C. if the insured dies during the 20-year term period, the monthly income is paid to the family for 20 years, starting at the time of death
    D. when the insured dies, the family generally may take the commuted value of the policy in cash in lieu of monthly income

38. Which of the following policy plans provides for payment of an income for a selected, fixed period of years beginning from the date of the insured's death?

    A. Family income
    B. Family maintenance
    C. Family plan
    D. Joint and survivor plan

39. Suppose that two years before he died, an insured bought a policy to maintain his family's income. The policy pays monthly benefits to the family for five years following the date of the insured's death. The face amount of the ordinary insurance portion of the policy is paid at the end of the five-year period. What kind of policy did the insured buy?

    A. Five-year family income plan
    B. Five-year family maintenance plan
    C. Seven-year family income plan
    D. Seven-year family maintenance plan

40. All of the following statements concerning a family plan policy are correct EXCEPT

    A. the policy normally is sold in units
    B. it typically covers all children in a family within certain age limits
    C. it provides both parents with the same amount of protection
    D. it is designed to insure all members of an immediate family in one policy

41. Don and Edith purchase a family plan consisting of four units to cover themselves and their two children. A unit provides coverage of $10,000 for Don, $2,500 for Edith and $2,000 for each child. Total coverage for each parent is

    A. $10,000 for Don and $2,500 for Edith
    B. $12,500 for Don and $10,000 for Edith
    C. $14,500 for Don and $2,500 for Edith
    D. $40,000 for Don and $10,000 for Edith

42. A family in which both parents work and, therefore, are in need of the same amount of coverage, would be a candidate for which of the following plans?

    A. Family maintenance
    B. Family plan
    C. Joint life
    D. Juvenile plan

43. All of the following statements pertaining to juvenile life insurance are correct EXCEPT

    A. Ricardo, father of Georgia, age six, has applied for a juvenile policy on his daughter's life. Ricardo will be the policyowner.
    B. Bobby, age eight, presently is the insured in a $5,000 "jumping juvenile" policy. When he reaches age 21, the policy's face amount automatically will increase to $25,000.
    C. Juvenile insurance may be purchased as soon as the child being insured can sign his or her name.
    D. The premiums for a "jumping juvenile" policy will remain level throughout the life of the policy.

44. The payor benefit typically waives premiums on a juvenile policy if the

    A. person who pays the premium dies or becomes disabled before the insured child reaches a certain age
    B. policy is converted before the insured reaches a specified age
    C. insured child becomes disabled
    D. insured child dies before reaching a specified age, usually 21 or 25

45. All of the following are purposes of juvenile insurance EXCEPT to

    A. provide funds for a child's final expenses
    B. fund a college education
    C. begin a life insurance program for a child at a low premium rate
    D. cover the medical expenses of a child

46. A significant feature of adjustable life insurance is that the

    A. policyowner may make retroactive adjustments in the policy's provisions
    B. premiums may be increased or decreased from time to time by the policyowner
    C. policyowner need not pay premiums after the policy has been in force for a certain number of years
    D. cash value is three times greater than in traditional whole life insurance

47. Patrick owns an adjustable life policy. Which of the following statements pertaining to his policy is CORRECT?

    A. Upon showing evidence of insurability, Patrick can increase the face amount of his policy.
    B. The company has a right to raise or lower the premium based on its investment earnings.
    C. Any adjustments made on the policy will have retroactive effects on the policy's provisions.
    D. Decreasing the premium shortens the premium-paying period.

48. Which of the following statements applies to universal life insurance?

    A. The policy involves a cash account and increasing term insurance coverage.
    B. A rate of interest higher than that paid on whole life is paid for the term of the policy.
    C. Premiums generally may be increased or decreased at the policyowner's option.
    D. It is similar to endowment insurance.

49. Universal life is distinguished from whole life insurance in that

    A. no withdrawals can be made from the policy's cash value account
    B. policy loans can be taken from the policy
    C. partial withdrawals can be taken from the cash value account
    D. complete withdrawals of the cash value can be taken

50. All of the following statements regarding universal life insurance are correct EXCEPT

    A. the policyowner has the right to increase or decrease the interest rate credited to his or her cash value account, as his or her needs change
    B. the cost of the insurance protection is taken from the policy's cash value account each month
    C. as long as the policy's cash values are sufficient to support the cost of the insurance protection and expenses, the policy remains in force, whether or not premiums are paid
    D. the policyowner has the right to increase or decrease the amount of the policy's death benefit, as his or her needs change

51. Michelle, age 31, just purchased a $50,000 variable life insurance policy. With regard to her policy, all of the following statements are correct EXCEPT

    A. Her premium payments will be fixed and level for the duration of the contract.
    B. She directs the insurer as to how her cash values are to be invested.
    C. The cash value growth of her policy will depend on how the investments supporting those values perform.
    D. At her death, her beneficiary may receive more or less than $50,000 in proceeds.

52. Which of the following types of life insurance requires that the agent be NASD-licensed before selling the policy?

    A. universal life
    B. variable life
    C. adjustable life
    D. term life

53. Which of the following statements pertaining to variable life insurance is CORRECT?

    A. The benefits of variable life insurance vary according to the amount of premiums paid.
    B. With a variable life insurance policy, the insurance company assumes the investment risk.
    C. Variable life insurance cannot be proposed in a sales situation unless the proposal is preceded or accompanied by a prospectus.
    D. In a variable life insurance policy, cash values and the death benefit are not guaranteed.

54. Variable universal life policies provide all of the following EXCEPT

    A. a flexible premium capability
    B. cash values
    C. a death benefit
    D. fixed premiums

55. Which of the following life insurance policy options will allow insureds to purchase additional insurance at future dates, regardless of their health?

    A. Guaranteed insurability option
    B. Double indemnity option
    C. Waiver of premium option
    D. Conversion option

56. At the age of 34, Ben purchased a whole life policy with a guaranteed insurability option. How many opportunities will he have to purchase additional life insurance in the future?

    A. Two
    B. Three
    C. Four
    D. Five

57. If an insured does not exercise his or her option to increase coverage under a guaranteed insurability rider, what is the result?

    A. The insurer automatically increases the coverage, per the amount stated in the option.
    B. The policy is canceled.
    C. The coverage will not change and the option automatically expires.
    D. The premiums on the underlying policy are lowered proportionately, since no increase in insurance coverage was purchased.

58. Jason has been totally disabled for two years. During that time, the company has paid all premiums (a total of $1,200) on his $25,000 life policy, which has a waiver of premium clause. If Jason dies now, the company will pay a death benefit of

    A. $12,500
    B. $23,300
    C. $23,800
    D. $25,000

59. All of the following statements pertaining to the waiver of premium provision in a life insurance policy are correct EXCEPT

    A. a waiver of premium provision specifies a waiting period of usually 90 days or six months after the disability commences before the waiver takes effect
    B. if the policy is participating, dividends will continue to be paid during the continuance of the disability
    C. after disability requirements are satisfied, premiums paid by the policyowner during the waiting period are refunded by the company
    D. a waiver of premium provision may be continued indefinitely with a policy so long as premiums are paid and the policy remains in force

60. Jay has a $50,000 life insurance policy with an accidental death benefit that pays triple the face amount. If Jay commits suicide three years after purchasing the policy, how much will his beneficiary receive?

    A. $0
    B. $50,000
    C. $100,000
    D. $150,000

61. For a beneficiary to receive accidental death benefits, death of the insured generally must occur within how many days following the accident?

    A. 30 days
    B. 45 days
    C. 60 days
    D. 90 days

62. The payor benefit option or rider is used with

    A. family income insurance
    B. joint life
    C. juvenile policies
    D. adjustable life

63. All of the following statements regarding a cost of living rider on a life insurance policy are correct EXCEPT

    A. A cost of living rider seeks to protect against inflation's erosion of life insurance policy values.
    B. An inflation index determines the amount of inflation adjustment that must be made to the policy up to a maximum percentage increase.
    C. All insurance companies offer cost of living riders.
    D. The cost of living rider provides increases in insurance without requiring the insured to provide evidence of insurability.

64. Upon the insured's death, which of the following policies will pay the face amount of the policy plus a sum equal to all or a portion of the premiums paid?

    A. Guaranteed dividend policy
    B. Adjusting benefit policy
    C. Cost of living policy
    D. Return of premium policy

65. What type of life insurance offers relatively small amounts of coverage for individuals who cannot typically afford larger policies?

    A. Group
    B. Industrial
    C. Whole
    D. Family

66. Which of the following kinds of life insurance is MOST widely used for group plans?

    A. Whole life
    B. Endowment
    C. Limited pay life
    D. Term

67. All of the following groups would be eligible for group insurance EXCEPT a(n)

    A. labor union
    B. employer-employee group
    C. family of 10
    D. trade association

68. Under a group life insurance plan, each insured person receives a(n)

    A. booklet of information
    B. insurance statement
    C. individual policy
    D. certificate of insurance

69. Group life insurance plans in which employees contribute to the overall premium are called

    A. group underwritten
    B. contributory
    C. participatory
    D. noncontributory

70. Television station KTKT has a group life policy covering its 90 employees, each of whom received a(n)

    A. certificate of insurance
    B. share of stock
    C. individual policy
    D. master policy

71. All of the following statements apply to franchise life insurance EXCEPT

    A. franchise plans are commonly used for large groups
    B. under a franchise plan, the type of insurance available to individual members is determined by the sponsoring association
    C. a franchise plan may provide for employer contributions
    D. a franchise plan deviates from the typical group plan in that the employer is not the master policyowner

72. Bob purchases a $50,000 five-year level term policy. All of the following statements about Bob's coverage are correct EXCEPT

    A. The policy provides a straight, level $50,000 of coverage for five years.
    B. If the insured dies at any time during the five years, his beneficiary will receive the policy's face value.
    C. If the insured dies after the specified five years, only the policy's cash value will be paid.
    D. If the insured lives beyond the five years, the policy expires and no benefits are payable.

73. Bob purchased a life insurance policy from a mutual insurer that has a low premium and face amount that diminishes after a few years. Policy dividends are used to buy paid-up additions to keep insurance equal to the amount of the reduction. What type of policy has Bob purchased?

    A. Indeterminate premium whole life
    B. Minimum deposit whole life
    C. Economatic whole life
    D. Indexed whole life

74. For a waiver of premium rider to become operative, the insured must be

    A. partially disabled
    B. totally disabled
    C. terminally ill
    D. chronically ill

Answers & Rationale

1.   B.   Under term life insurance, the option to renew allows the policyowner to renew the policy without evidence of insurability. The renewal is then effected by the policyowner paying the premium for the age then attained, not per the basis of his or her health.
QID: 1128

2.   C.   Under a renewable term policy, the premiums remain level for each term period, but increase at each renewal based on the older age of the insured.
QID: 1129

3.   C.   Nonrenewable policies are less expensive than renewable policies, all other things being equal. This is because the renewal provision provides continued coverage without evidence of insurability, putting the insurer at greater risk.
QID: 1130

4.   A.   Under term life insurance, the option to convert offers the insured the right to change the term policy to permanent insurance without evidence of insurability.
QID: 1131

5.   D.   A term policy can be purchased with an option to renew, an option to convert or both. The option to renew allows the policyowner to renew the policy (at the then-attained age premium) without evidence of insurability. The option to convert allows the policyowner to convert the term policy to a permanent type (with an adjustment to premium), without evidence of insurability. Renewable policies carry higher premiums than nonrenewable policies.
QID: 1132

6.   B.   The option to renew and the option to convert are available in term insurance for additional premiums.
QID: 1133

7.   C.   Level term insurance provides a level face amount of coverage for the term of the policy. Because it covers a specified term only (and does not have a cash value), it is cheaper than whole and limited pay (including single-premium) life. Since the $150,000 amount remains level in this problem, level term insurance is just what is needed.
QID: 1134

8.   D.   Level term insurance provides a constant, level face amount of coverage for the term of the policy.
QID: 1135

9.   B.   If Peggy dies within the 10-year term period, her beneficiaries will equally split the $50,000 face amount, each receiving $25,000.
QID: 1136

10.   D.   In this case, the insured died after his term policy period had expired. As a result, his beneficiary received nothing.
QID: 1137

11.   B.   Level term insurance provides a fixed, level face amount. Decreasing term insurance provides a constantly decreasing benefit amount and carries a lower premium. As a result, Chester's beneficiary would have received $25,000 from his level term policy, and Joel's beneficiary would have received less from his decreasing term policy, had both insureds died within the 15-year term periods. However, if death took place after 1999 (the end of the 15-year term period), neither Chester's nor Joel's beneficiary would receive anything.
QID: 1138

12.   D.   Decreasing term insurance is designed to address needs which decrease from year to year, such as mortgage or loan protection. By the end of the term period, the face amount decreases to nothing. This would not help create a retirement fund.
QID: 1139

13.   B.   Decreasing term insurance is designed to address needs which decrease from year to year. A decreasing term policy could be written for an amount of insurance to equal the remaining cost of the son's tuition. It would not be used as a method to create funds as would be necessary to fund the daughter's education, nor does it create any cash value that could be borrowed.
QID: 1140

14.   B.   Increasing term insurance is used primarily to provide a benefit that increases over time. As such, it is usually sold as a rider.
QID: 1141

15.   C.   Credit life is usually sold in the form of decreasing term insurance. In this way, the policy amount decreases to zero when the loan is paid.
QID: 1142

16.   A.   The accumulation that builds over the life of a policy is referred to as the policy's cash value, and belongs to the policyowner, who may or may not be the insured.
QID: 1143

17.   A.   The cash values of a straight whole life policy can be accessed through a policy loan or through a complete withdrawal of the entire cash value. A policy loan allows the policy to continue in force (though any amount not paid back with interest at the time of death will be subtracted from the death benefit); a complete withdrawal constitutes a surrender of the policy and coverage would lapse.
QID: 1144

18.   A.   The cash values of a whole life policy grow steadily and, if the insured lives and premiums are paid to age 100, will equal the face amount.
QID: 1145

19.   D.   The face amount of a whole life policy may be paid as a lump sum at the policyowner's death, not at retirement age.
QID: 1146

20.   D.   An option to renew is a feature of term insurance.
QID: 1147

21.   C.   Upon the death of an insured, a whole life policy pays its face amount. In this case, the face amount is $100,000.
QID: 1148

22.   B.   Term policies do not "endow" (meaning the point when the cash value equals the face amount). Endowment policies can endow at different ages. Whole life and limited pay life endow at age 100.
QID: 1149

23.   B.   By design, a whole life policy endows for its face amount at age 100. That means at the policyowner's age 100 the values of his or her policy equal the face amount of the policy. At that point, the insurance is canceled, and the insured receives the face amount as an endowment.
QID: 1150

24.   B.   Both limited pay life and whole life policies endow at age 100. A single-premium policy would cost less than a policy with payments spread over its term, since there are fewer administrative expenses involved with single payment policy.
QID: 1151

25.   A.   Limited pay life insurance policies have shorter premium-paying periods. The shorter the period, the higher the premium.
QID: 1152

26.   C.   Although the premium payments are limited to a certain period, the insurance protection extends until the insured's death or to age 100.
QID: 1153

27.   A.   The endowment described in this question is a 20-year endowment and, as such, necessitates 20 years of premiums.
QID: 1154

28. A. The policy described in this question is a 20-pay endowment at age 60. The premiums are payable for 20 years and the policy endows at the insured's age 60.
QID: 1155

29. D. A 30-year endowment policy provides 30 years of insurance protection.
QID: 1156

30. D. The policy described is a 20-pay endowment at age 60 policy. In this case, the premium payments are paid for 20 years before the time of endowment.
QID: 1157

31. C. The modified whole life policy is a variation of the traditional whole life policy, not an endowment policy. The premiums in a modified whole life policy are lower in the early years of the policy's term and higher in its later years.
QID: 1158

32. B. The modified whole life policy is issued with a level premium payable during the first few (usually five) years that is lower than the normal whole life policy rates. The premium increases and is higher than normal thereafter.
QID: 1159

33. C. Graded premium whole life, like modified whole life, redistributes the policy premiums. The premium is lower than normal whole life rates during the preliminary period following issue (usually five to ten years) and increases each year until leveling off after the preliminary period. A modified whole life policy has a level premium during the preliminary period.
QID: 1160

34. A. Premiums for modified whole life policies do not increase annually after the first few years. They level off after the premium period.
QID: 1161

35. C. The face amount of an indexed whole life policy increases automatically when the Consumer Price Index increases. Either the policyowner or the insurer assumes the risk and pays the additional premium with each face amount increase. If the policyowner assumes the risk, he or she pays the additional premium. If the insurer assumes the risk, the insurer pays. In either case, the policyowner is not required to furnish evidence of insurability to obtain the face amount increase.
QID: 1162

36. C. When Congress enacted The Technical and Miscellaneous Revenue Act (TAMRA), it effectively created a new class of insurance called modified endowment contracts (MECs). MECs are taxed differently than other insurance policies. If the total amount a policyowner pays into a life contract during its first years exceeds the sum of the net level premiums that would have been payable to provide paid-up future benefits in seven years, the policy is classified as an MEC. If the policyowner receives any amount from an MEC as a loan or withdrawal, that amount will be taxed first as ordinary income and second as a return of premium. Plus, there is a 10 percent penalty tax on amounts taken if the policyowner has not reached age 59 ½.
QID: 1163

37. C. If the insured dies during the 20-year term period, the monthly income would be paid from the time of the insured's death until the end of the remainder of the term, not for a full 20 years.
QID: 1164

38. B. Family maintenance policies use level term insurance to provide for payment of an income for a selected, fixed period beginning at the insured's death.
QID: 1165

39. B. A family maintenance plan, which uses a level term rider, provides for payment of income for a selected, fixed period of years that begins from the date of death. The face amount of the ordinary insurance portion of the contract is paid at the end of the fixed period. In this case, the term for which monthly benefits will be paid is five years.
QID: 1166

40. C. Family plan policies are designed for a one-income family where most of the insurance is placed on the wage earner. The policies are normally sold in units and cover all members of the family.
QID: 1167

41. D. The number of units in a family plan is multiplied by the amount of coverage. As a result, Don receives $40,000; Edith, $10,000.
QID: 1168

42. C. A joint life plan is simply one policy covering two or more persons. Usually, permanent insurance is written.
QID: 1169

43. C. Insurance written on the lives of children, who ordinarily are from one day to 14 or 15 years old, is called "juvenile insurance." An adult, usually a parent or a grandparent, applies for, pays for and owns the policy until the child is old enough to carry the premiums personally. A special kind of juvenile policy, described in the second answer choice, is known as a "jumping juvenile" policy. This type of policy is issued on a child in units of $1,000, and automatically increases to five times the originally issued face amount when the child reaches age 21.
QID: 1170

44. A. The payor provision provides that in the event of the premium payor's death or disability, premiums on the policy will be waived until the insured child attains a specified age or until the maturity date of the contract, whichever occurs first.
QID: 1171

45. D. Juvenile insurance may provide funds for a child's final expenses, for a college education or to begin a life insurance program for a child, at relatively low premium rates. Juvenile insurance also can assure a child has some life insurance if he or she becomes uninsurable later.
QID: 1172

46. B. An adjustable life policy is simply a whole life policy with adjustable features, such as premiums which may be increased or decreased from time to time by the policyowner. Such adjustments cannot be made retroactively.
QID: 1173

47. A. Adjustable life is a whole life policy with adjustable features. Premiums may be increased or decreased at the policyowner's request as can the face amount of the policy (usually subject to evidence of insurability). None of the changes made in an adjustable life policy has any retroactive effect on any of the provisions; adjustments apply only to the future. Increasing the premiums could lengthen the coverage period or shorten the premium-paying period. Decreasing the premiums reduces cash values, shortens the protection period or lengthens the premium-paying period.
QID: 1174

48. C. Universal life insurance functions as whole life insurance but is essentially level or decreasing term insurance plus an investment account. It matches a client's needs in that he or she can adjust premium payments, the face amount of the policy, or both. Interest is based on the greater of the current rate or the guaranteed policy minimum.
QID: 1175

49. C. A factor that distinguishes universal life from whole life is that partial withdrawals can be made from the policy's cash value account. Whole life insurance allows a policyowner to tap cash values only through a policy loan or a complete cash surrender of the policy's cash values, in which case the policy terminates.
QID: 1176

50. A. With a universal life insurance policy, an insured can increase the death benefit of the policy as needs dictate; no new policy is issued. Premium payments may be increased, decreased or skipped altogether as long as the cash values are sufficient to pay the monthly premiums. The death benefit is not reduced when premiums are

paid from cash values. The amount of interest credited to the policy is the guaranteed rate plus any excess earned.
QID: 1177

51. D. A variable life insurance policy invests its cash values in securities at the owner's direction. There are no guarantees as to the cash value growth or accumulation. Although the death benefit may fluctuate in response to the cash values, a minimum death benefit—the policy's face amount—is guaranteed. Premiums are fixed and payable over the life of the policy.
QID: 1178

52. B. To sell variable life insurance, an individual must hold a life insurance producer's license and a National Association of Securities Dealers (NASD) registered representative's license.
QID: 1179

53. C. Because variable life insurance is considered a security, a prospectus must precede any sale of it.
QID: 1180

54. D. Variable universal life insurance combines many characteristics of variable life (such as a death benefit and an equities-based cash value) with universal life (such as flexible premium payments and adjustable death benefits).
QID: 1181

55. A. The guaranteed insurability option (or rider) permits the insured, at stated intervals, to buy specified amounts of additional insurance without evidence of insurability. The option requires an additional premium and is usually attached to a permanent life policy at the time of purchase.
QID: 1182

56. A. Typically, the guaranteed insurability option allows the insured to purchase additional insurance at three-year intervals between ages 25 and 40. In this case, Ben would be able to exercise this option at age 37 and at age 40.
QID: 1183

57. C. When no purchase is made under a guaranteed insurability option, the option for that particular age expires automatically. There is no change in the underlying policy. Normally, the insured will have 90 days in which to exercise an optional purchase.
QID: 1184

58. D. Although premiums are waived due to the waiver of premium clause, the death benefit ($25,000) remains the same.
QID: 1185

59. D. A waiver of premium clause generally remains in effect until the insured reaches a specified age, such as 60 or 65.
QID: 1186

60. B. Suicide is excluded from coverage under the accidental death benefit and, as a result, does not qualify for the additional payment.
QID: 1187

61. D. For a beneficiary to receive accidental death benefits, death of the insured generally must occur within 90 days following an accident.
QID: 1188

62. C. The juvenile policy's payor benefit rider provides that the policy premiums will be waived if the person paying the premium dies or becomes totally disabled.
QID: 1190

63. C. A cost of living (COL) or cost of living adjustment (COLA) rider is tied to an increase in an inflation index, most commonly the Consumer Price Index (CPI). The COL rider provides for automatic increases in the policy death benefit in proportion to increases in the CPI.
QID: 1193

64. D. Return of premium policies promise to pay the policy face amount plus a sum equal to all or a portion of the premiums paid. Usually the return is limited to premiums paid during a stated period, such as 10 or 15 years, or to a stated age,

such as 60. Of course, these policies are more expensive than those that do not have a return of premium guarantee.
QID: 1194

65.   B.   Industrial life is often called "burial insurance" because of its small policy limits and corresponding small premiums.
QID: 1195

66.   D.   Most group life insurance plans offer term insurance because of the lower cost factor to the employer.
QID: 1196

67.   C.   Family members are not considered groups for the purposes of group insurance.
QID: 1198

68.   D.   Under a group life insurance plan, each insured employee receives a certificate of insurance. The employer receives the actual policy and is the policyowner.
QID: 1199

69.   B.   When employees contribute to the premium payable for a group life insurance contract, the plan is called contributory.
QID: 1293

70.   A.   Employee members of the group receive a certificate of insurance. The company, as policyowner, received a master policy.
QID: 1294

71.   A.   Franchise life plans are commonly used for small groups whose numbers are less than the minimum required by state law for group insurance coverage.
QID: 1296

72.   C.   If the insured lives beyond the five-year period, the policy expires and no benefits are payable. There are no cash values in term policies.QID: 3314

73.   C.   Bob purchased an economatic whole life policy. A mutual company issues this type of policy with a low premium and face amount that diminishes after a few years. Dividends are used to buy paid-up additions to keep insurance equal to the amount of the reduction. In this manner, the face amount remains constant.
QID: 3315

74.   B.   An insured must be totally disabled for a waiver of premium rider to become operative. The policyowner does not have to pay premiums as long as the disability continues. Instead, the company continues to pay all premiums that become due while the insured's disability continues.
QID: 3316

6

Premiums and Proceeds

1. If the employer pays the entire premium on a group policy, the plan is called

   A. contributory
   B. noncontributory
   C. industrial
   D. convertible

2. What tool do life insurance actuaries use to help establish premium rates based on the probabilities of death at various ages?

   A. Morbidity table
   B. Mortality table
   C. Survivor table
   D. Annuity table

3. A mortality table reflects

   A. the average life-span for any given individual
   B. who among a given group of individuals will die within a given year
   C. the average number of deaths that will occur in a given year for a given age group of individuals
   D. the declining probability of death as the age of a given group of individuals increases

4. Suppose that out of a starting group of 100,000 individuals, 89,666 are living at age 50 and 902 are expected to die within the year. What is the death rate for that particular age group?

   A. 1 percent
   B. 10 percent
   C. 20 percent
   D. 29 percent

5. In the life insurance business, a word that is synonymous with "expenses" is

   A. underwriting
   B. loading
   C. actuary
   D. controlling

6. All of the following statements pertaining to life insurance premiums are correct EXCEPT

   A. an insurance company invests the premium money it collects to earn interest
   B. in establishing premium rates, a company must assume it will earn a high rate of interest on its invested premiums
   C. the expense factor in premium rate-making frequently is referred to as "loading"
   D. for an insurance company, the costs of doing business must be reflected in its premiums

7. An insurer invests the premiums it receives in order to earn interest. Which of the following statements regarding this interest factor is CORRECT?

   A. It is factored into the premium rates the insurer charges, which keeps those rates lower than they would be if there were no interest earnings.
   B. The rate of return the insurer earns on its invested premiums is the rate it guarantees its policies will pay.
   C. The higher the assumed rate of interest, the higher the premium rate charged to policyowners.
   D. In calculating the interest, it is assumed that all premiums are paid at the end of the year.

8. Which of the following statements pertaining to life insurance premiums is CORRECT?

   A. Bob, who is substantially overweight, has applied for a life insurance policy. His weight may affect his insurability, but not the amount of the premium on his policy.
   B. Harold and Billy, both age 25, each buy a whole life policy from the same company. However, Harold has a participating policy, while Billy's policy is nonparticipating. Harold will pay a higher premium.
   C. All life insurance companies charge the same premiums for smokers and non-smokers.
   D. The three factors that affect the basic premium are preexisting conditions, interest and expense.

9. Which of the following age groups normally experiences the LARGEST number of deaths in a year?

   A. 20-year-olds
   B. 30-year-olds
   C. 40-year-olds
   D. 50-year-olds

10. All of the following are basic premium factors EXCEPT

    A. the insurer's expenses
    B. interest earnings
    C. the insured's annual income
    D. the mortality rate

11. All of the following can affect directly the amount of premium an individual insured pays EXCEPT

    A. occupation
    B. sex
    C. age
    D. marital status

12. Assume the following persons buy identical life insurance policies from the same company. Who would pay the lowest premium rate?

    A. Linda, age 30
    B. Thomas, age 30
    C. Brandon, age 34
    D. Arthur, age 42

13. Which of the following types of life insurance policies would have premiums that are fixed and level, and payable over the life of the policy?

    A. Life paid-up at 50
    B. 10-year renewable term
    C. Indexed whole life
    D. Single-premium whole life

14. Ben is considering the purchase of a $75,000 whole life policy. Which of the following options would tend to lower his premiums?

    A. The addition of a guaranteed insurability rider
    B. The waiver of premium option
    C. Paying premiums annually as opposed to monthly
    D. The addition of a cost of living rider

15. A life insurance gross premium is

    A. net single premium plus mortality
    B. interest plus expense less mortality
    C. net single premium plus expense
    D. mortality costs plus loading

16. When establishing premiums, insurers express the rate as a

    A. percentage of the policy's face amount
    B. flat rate per risk
    C. cost per insured individual
    D. cost per $1,000 of face amount

17. All of the following factors influence an applicant's mortality EXCEPT

    A. Hazardous occupation
    B. Personal habits
    C. Dangerous hobby
    D. Credit report

18. The annual premium on Rhoda's life insurance policy came due December 1, 2000. She paid the premium, which was for

    A. 1999
    B. 2000
    C. 2001
    D. any year she designates

19. The funds set aside by an insurer to cover future claims on its life insurance policies is known as the

    A. guaranty fund
    B. reserve
    C. surplus
    D. asset account

20. What settlement option is designed to pay out a specified amount of income at regular intervals, over an unspecified period of time?

    A. Fixed period option
    B. Interest-only option
    C. Life income option
    D. Fixed amount option

21. Suppose Max wants to arrange the distribution of his life insurance proceeds so that his wife, as beneficiary, will receive monthly payments for as long as she lives. Which of the following settlement options will meet this need?

    A. Fixed-period option
    B. Fixed-amount option
    C. Interest-only option
    D. Life income option

22. As beneficiary, Kathryn receives $800 monthly from her deceased husband's life insurance under a fixed amount option. Each payment consists partly of principal (proceeds) and partly of interest. How is this income taxed?

A. Each payment is received fully tax free.
B. The portion of each payment consisting of principal is taxed; the remainder is tax free.
C. The portion of each payment consisting of interest is taxed; the remainder is tax free.
D. Each payment is fully taxed.

23. In which of the following situations would premium payments be tax deductible?

A. Randy is the owner and premium payer of a life insurance policy covering his wife, Ellen.
B. Janet is the owner and premium payer of a mortgage policy that covers the outstanding mortgage on her home.
C. The ABC Company provides $25,000 of life insurance coverage to each of its 15 employees and pays the full premium.
D. The ABC Company is the owner and premium payer of a $250,000 key executive policy covering the life of its president.

24. With regard to the taxation of life insurance policies, which of the following statements is CORRECT?

A. Amy owns a participating life insurance policy on her own life. She can deduct the premium payments, but she will be taxed on any dividends the policy may pay.
B. Terry owns a 10-year old whole life insurance policy which she surrenders for cash. She will be taxed on the full amount she receives, since the policy did not mature.
C. The premiums that Acme Manufacturing pays for its business life insurance policies (key purpose insurance, entity cross-purchase plans) are tax deductible.
D. As long as a whole life policy is not surrendered, the cash value accumulates tax free.

25. Which of the following settlement options produces benefits that are fully income tax exempt to life insurance beneficiaries?

A. Fixed-amount benefits
B. Lump-sum payments
C. Fixed-period benefits
D. Interest-only payments

26. Archibald surrenders a life insurance policy and receives a lump-sum cash payment of $32,000. His premium payments up to the time of surrender amounted to $26,000. How is the surrender treated for tax purposes?

A. The full $32,000 is received tax free.
B. Archibald will receive $6,000 tax free and will be taxed on his $26,000 cost basis.
C. Archibald will receive his $26,000 cost basis tax free and will be taxed on $6,000.
D. The full $32,000 is taxable as ordinary income.

27. Renee is the owner and insured of a $100,000 policy. She sells the policy to her business partner, Jill, for $35,000 and for the next ten years, Jill pays the $1,200 annual premium. Assuming Renee dies 10 years after the transfer and the $100,000 is paid to Jill, how are the proceeds taxed under the transfer-for-value rule?

   A. Jill receives the $100,000 tax free.
   B. Jill will be taxed on $65,000, the difference between what she paid for the policy and the proceeds she received.
   C. Jill will be taxed on $53,000, the difference between what she paid for the policy plus the premiums she paid, and the proceeds she received.
   D. Jill will be taxed on the $100,000. The transfer-for-value rule makes policies sold for consideration fully taxable.

28. Assume Silo, Inc., provides each of its 20 employees with $50,000 in group term life insurance coverage. Which of the following statements is CORRECT?

   A. Silo, Inc., can deduct the cost of the premiums as a business expense.
   B. Each Silo employee must report his or her proportional share of the premium as income.
   C. Silo, Inc., cannot deduct the cost of the premiums it pays for its group life coverage.
   D. Any lump-sum proceeds paid under the Silo group life plan to a deceased employee's beneficiary are taxable as income.

29. Lynn elects to surrender her whole life policy for a reduced paid-up policy. The cash value of her new policy will

   A. continue to increase
   B. remain the same as in the old policy
   C. reduce immediately to $0
   D. decrease gradually

30. Basil has a combination policy consisting of $25,000 whole life and a $20,000 term rider. He stops paying premiums and elects to take a paid-up policy, which will be a reduced amount of insurance based on an original face amount of

   A. $20,000
   B. $25,000
   C. $35,000
   D. $45,000

31. John, age 52, has a straight whole life policy and decides to stop paying premiums and take a paid-up policy for a reduced amount. His paid-up policy will be

   A. any type of policy he selects
   B. an annuity
   C. whole life
   D. term insurance

32. A policyowner stops paying premiums on a whole life policy with an accidental death benefit and exchanges the policy for extended term insurance. All of the following statements pertaining to this situation are correct EXCEPT

   A. the term policy will have a reduced face value
   B. the policyowner will have continued protection for a limited period of time
   C. the term policy has no cash value
   D. there will be no accidental death benefit with the new policy

33. At age 60, Durwood decides to stop paying premiums on his $60,000 whole life policy, and exchanges it for extended term insurance. What face value will the term insurance have?

   A. $10,000
   B. $30,000
   C. $45,000
   D. $60,000

34. Arnold buys a $25,000 participating whole life policy. He has a definite need for more life insurance, but believes he cannot afford it. Which of the following dividend options would help to solve this problem automatically?

    A. Taking dividends in cash
    B. Applying dividends against premium payments
    C. Using dividends to buy paid-up additions
    D. Leaving dividends to accumulate at interest

35. All of the following are dividend options EXCEPT

    A. buying paid-up additions
    B. applying dividends to premiums
    C. assigning dividends to pay off a mortgage
    D. leaving dividends to accumulate at interest

36. Unlike corporate dividends, insurance policy dividends

    A. are reported on an insured's income tax filing
    B. are the same as marketable securities
    C. are not considered taxable income
    D. are guaranteed to be declared and payable every year

37. Which of the following dividend options produces a result similar to taking dividends in cash and depositing them in a bank savings account?

    A. Using dividends to buy one-year term insurance
    B. Leaving dividends to accumulate at interest
    C. Applying dividends against premium payments
    D. Taking dividends in cash

38. Which of the following statements is CORRECT with regard to policy dividends?

    A. They are issued on nonparticipating policies.
    B. They are a result of favorable operating or investment income.
    C. Though they may vary from year to year, they are guaranteed to be paid each year.
    D. They are not available to insureds after a specified age, such as 60.

39. As primary beneficiary under a cash refund option in a life insurance policy, Jeffrey received $355 per month for five years before suffering a fatal heart attack. The policy's original proceeds amounted to $50,000. Jeffrey's daughter, the secondary beneficiary, will now receive

    A. a lump-sum payment of $28,700
    B. $355 per month, as payments continue in her name
    C. a lump sum payment of $50,000
    D. nothing

40. Horace wants his $85,000 life insurance policy arranged to pay his wife a monthly income if he dies first, but most or all of the proceeds to go to their two children after her death. Which of the following settlement options could Horace select to provide income for his wife and conserve the proceeds for the children?

    A. Interest-only option
    B. Fixed-period option
    C. Fixed-amount option
    D. Life income option

41. Once a life insurance settlement option has been put into effect, the relationship between a beneficiary and the insurance company is that of

    A. recipient/donor
    B. payee/trustee
    C. creditor/debtor
    D. heir/grantor

42. All of the following statements pertaining to life insurance policy settlement options are correct EXCEPT

   A. By using the interest-only option, two or more settlement options can be combined for added flexibility.
   B. Payments under the interest-only option may be made at a rate higher than the guaranteed minimum.
   C. Diane and Rhonda were receiving monthly income from identical life insurance policies under the fixed-period option. Diane's payments were for 15 years and Rhonda's for 20 years. Diane received the larger payments.
   D. Under a life income option, income payments will continue as long as the primary beneficiary lives or until the principal is depleted.

43. Under a fixed-period life insurance settlement option, excess interest will

   A. increase the size of the payments
   B. shorten the payment period
   C. have no effect on payments
   D. lengthen the payment period

44. Which of the following statements pertaining to life insurance policy settlement options is CORRECT?

   A. Excess interest reduces the amount of each income payment under a fixed-amount option.
   B. Under a fixed-amount option, the lower the interest rate, the smaller each payment will be.
   C. Selection of a smaller payment will increase the payment period under a fixed-amount option.
   D. Principal and interest are paid over a specified number of years under a fixed-amount option.

45. Which of the following descriptions of life insurance policy settlement options is CORRECT?

   A. Under a life-income-only option, if a primary beneficiary dies after receiving income payments for only three months, the balance of the proceeds would be paid in a lump sum to the secondary beneficiary.
   B. Glenn chooses a life-income-only option and Jerry a life income with cash refund option. Jerry's income is based on the higher rate per $1,000 of proceeds.
   C. Under an installment refund option, if the primary beneficiary dies, payments of the same amount continue to the secondary beneficiary until all installments to both beneficiaries equal the original amount of proceeds.
   D. Today, most life insurance proceeds are paid out as a lump sum.

46. Beth is secondary beneficiary of a life policy, receiving monthly income benefits under an installment refund option. Her mother, the primary beneficiary, received a total of $4,200 in benefits before she died. The original proceeds totaled $22,000. Assuming Beth lives long enough, she will be paid monthly benefits until she has received a total of

   A. $4,200
   B. $17,800
   C. $18,700
   D. $22,000

47. Under an installment refund settlement option, if the primary beneficiary dies, the secondary beneficiary will receive

   A. a lump-sum payment
   B. the same income payments until the total amount paid out to both beneficiaries equals the original amount of proceeds
   C. one-half of the remaining proceeds
   D. the same income payments for a fixed period of years

48. Norris is the primary beneficiary of a life insurance policy. He dies after receiving $275 per month for six years, under a 10-year period certain income option. His son, Neil, is the secondary beneficiary. Which of the following statements pertaining to this situation is CORRECT?

    A. Neil will receive income checks in the same amount as his father for four years.
    B. Neil will receive $275 monthly for as long as he lives.
    C. Neil will receive nothing since Norris did not survive the ten-year period certain.
    D. Neil will receive a lump-sum payment of $13,200.

49. Which of the following period certain income options would call for the highest payment rate per $1,000 of life policy proceeds?

    A. 15-year period certain
    B. 10-year period certain
    C. 5-year period certain
    D. 20-year period certain

50. Hector's wife was the primary beneficiary of his $250,000 life insurance policy. She received payments of approximately $700 a month as long as she lived and, at her death, their two children received lump-sum payments of $125,000 each. What settlement option was in effect on Hector's policy?

    A. Life income option
    B. Interest-only option
    C. Period certain option
    D. Installment refund option

51. Doris and Arnold receive $450 per month under a joint and one-half survivor life insurance option. What happens if Arnold should die first after payments are started?

    A. Doris would receive $450 per month as long as she lived.
    B. Doris would have to select another settlement option.
    C. The remaining proceeds would be paid to Doris in a lump sum.
    D. Monthly payments of $225 would be made to Doris as long as she lived.

52. Carl and Laura receive $270 per month under a joint and two-thirds survivor life policy settlement option. What would happen if Carl died within one year after payment started?

    A. The balance of the proceeds would be paid to Laura in a lump sum.
    B. Laura would receive $135 per month for as long as she lived.
    C. Laura would continue to receive a monthly benefit of $270 for as long as she lived.
    D. Laura would receive $180 per month for as long as she lived.

53. What is the method used for establishing a premium for group insurance?

    A. Enrollment rating
    B. Group credit rating
    C. Experience rating
    D. Franchise rating

54. In which of the following situations can the premium payor of a life insurance policy deduct the premium payments for tax purposes?

A. Joe, the sole proprietor of a grocery store, purchases and pays premiums on a $75,000 term life policy on his life and names his wife as beneficiary.
B. Leland, a local board member of the United Way, assigns his $25,000 whole life policy to that organization, but continues to make the premium payments.
C. Michelle, the legal guardian of five-year-old Angela, makes the premium payments on Angela's $5,000 juvenile life insurance policy.
D. Bob takes over the premium payments on his son's $30,000 whole life policy after his son declares bankruptcy.

55. Which of the following premium factors has the greatest effect on life insurance premium calculations?

A. mortality
B. interest
C. expense
D. health

Answers & Rationale

1. B. When the employer pays the whole premium for a group life insurance plan, it is called "noncontributory."
QID: 1197

2. B. A mortality table is used to help establish life insurance premium rates, since it helps actuaries predict the number of deaths and thus, the number of insurance claims an insurer could expect to experience in any given year. Morbidity tables predict disabilities.
QID: 1200

3. C. A mortality table reflects the average number of deaths that will occur in a certain year for a given group of people. "Mortality" is the relative incidence of death within a given group.
QID: 1201

4. A. The death rate, also known as the prediction of mortality, is expressed as the percentage of those living who are expected to die within a year. Thus, 902 divided by 89,666 equals 1 percent. One percent of 50-year-olds would be expected to die during the year.
QID: 1202

5. B. Each premium an insurer charges must carry its small proportion of normal operating expenses. The expense factor is computed and included in the premium rates for life insurance. The expense factor is also called the "loading charge."
QID: 1203

6. B. A company must remain conservative (low) in its interest earnings assumption. The company is committed to the interest rate it guaranteed its policies will pay.
QID: 1204

7. A. The interest the insurer earns on invested premiums is factored into the premium rates it charges, so that the rate charged is lower than it would be if no interest earnings were assumed. The rate of interest the insurer earns on invested premiums is not the rate it guarantees on its policies. In fact, insurers hope the return they earn will be higher than what they pay, in order to realize a profit. It is assumed that all premiums are paid at the beginning of the year.
QID: 1205

8. B. Participating policies pay dividends. A higher premium must be charged for a participating policy since it provides dividends. Insurability, as affected by the overweight applicant in the first answer choice, directly affects premium amounts. The three factors that affect the basic premium are mortality, interest and expense.
QID: 1206

9. D. For obvious reasons, older people die in greater proportions. Thus, the older the age group, the higher the death rate for that group.
QID: 1207

10. C. Three basic factors must be considered when computing the premium rate for a life insurance policy mortality (the event or risk the insured wants to protect against); interest (the amount assumed to be earned on the insurer's funds); and expenses (the overhead charges the insurer incurs).
QID: 1208

11. D. For any one individual, occupation, age and sex are factors considered in developing a life insurance premium. Marital status is not, since it does not directly affect a person's proposed life span.
QID: 1209

12. A. Since female mortality rates are generally lower than those for males, a 30-year-old woman would pay less for life insurance than a 30-year-old man.
QID: 1210

13. B. Both the life paid-up at 50 and the 10-year renewable term have fixed, level premiums. However, with the life paid-up at 50, though the coverage extends to the insured's age 100, premiums cease when he or she is 50. The 10-year renewable term would require premium payments for the full 10-year period, after which the coverage would end unless renewed. Premiums for indexed-whole life policies fluctuate according to the Consumer Price Index. A single-premium whole life policy is paid with one large premium at the beginning of the policy.
QID: 1211

14. C. The less frequently premiums are collected on a life insurance policy, the less it costs the insurer to administer that policy and the more the insurer will have to invest. Consequently, an annual premium payment mode would be less expensive than a monthly premium payment mode. Options that add value to a policy, like guaranteed insurability, waiver of premium and cost of living rider, would tend to increase the cost of the policy.
QID: 1212

15. C. A life insurance gross premium is the amount a policyowner is expected to pay. It is comprised of the single amount needed to fund the future benefit (net single premium) and normal operating costs associated with providing coverage (expense).
QID: 1213

16. D. Premium rates for life insurance are expressed as an annual cost per $1,000 of face amount. Thus, if the cost is $12 per $1,000, the annual premium for a $50,000 policy would be $600 ($12 x 50).
QID: 1214

17. D. Those employed in hazardous occupations pose a greater risk to an insurer, as do those who engage in dangerous hobbies, such as skydiving. Habits such as smoking or overeating can also increase the risk of death.
QID: 1215

18. C. All life insurance premiums are payable in advance. Thus, a premium due on December 1, 2000 was applied to 2001.
QID: 1216

19. B. The reserve is the amount, when combined with future premiums and interest, that will be used to cover an insurer's death claims. A life insurer's reserve is considered a liability, because it represents an obligation the insurer must fulfill.
QID: 1218

20. D. The fixed amount settlement option provides for the payment of a policy's death benefit in specified amounts at regular intervals. The duration of the payments is not specified; payments are made until the proceeds—or principal—and interest are exhausted.
QID: 1219

21. D. The life income option provides for the guaranteed payment of the proceeds for the life of the beneficiary.
QID: 1220

22. C. The monthly payment to the beneficiary under the fixed amount option is considered a partially taxable installment (similar to an annuity payment). A fixed, unchanged portion of each payment is considered a return of principal and is therefore tax free. The balance, however, is taxable as interest income.
QID: 1221

23. C. Premiums paid by a company for group term life insurance are deductible as a business expense, assuming the group plan and its provisions meet the necessary requirements. Premiums paid for personal life insurance are not tax deductible, including key person insurance.
QID: 1222

24. D. Premium payments for personal and business life insurance are not deductible and dividends paid on participating policies are not taxable. Policy surrenders are taxable only to the extent that amounts received exceed total premiums paid by the policyowner.
QID: 1223

25.   B.   The lump-sum payment settlement option produces death benefits that are fully income tax exempt to life insurance beneficiaries. The other options involve interest earned on the proceeds, which is not tax exempt.
QID: 1224

26.   C.   Archibald will be taxed on the amount that exceeds the $26,000 he paid into the policy, his cost basis.
QID: 1225

27.   A.   The transfer-for-value rule states that if a policy is transferred for consideration and the insured dies, the transferee will be taxed on the excess of the proceeds over the consideration, including any premiums. However, this rule does not apply to transfers to a partner of the insured.
QID: 1226

28.   A.   The premiums paid for the first $50,000 of employer-provided group term life insurance coverage are not taxable to the employee. The employer may deduct these costs as a business expense. Proceeds are never taxable as income if they are paid in a lump sum.
QID: 1227

29.   A.   Once Lynn surrendered her whole life policy for a reduced paid-up policy, the face value is reduced but cash values continue to increase.
QID: 1255

30.   B.   A reduced paid-up policy is based on the original whole life policy amount; the term rider amount is not considered.
QID: 1256

31.   C.   When a policyowner decides to stop paying premiums and take a paid-up policy for a reduced amount, the paid-up policy will be the same kind as the original policy.
QID: 1257

32.   A.   When a policyowner stops paying premiums on a whole life policy with an accidental death benefit and exchanges the policy for extended term insurance, a policy's cash surrender value is used to purchase an amount of term insurance equal to the original policy's face amount. The term insurance will last as long as the cash value is sufficient to pay premiums. An accidental death benefit would not be included.
QID: 1258

33.   D.   When a policyowner stops paying premiums on a whole life policy and exchanges the policy for extended term insurance, a policy's cash surrender value is used to purchase an amount of term insurance equal to the original policy's face amount. The term insurance will last as long as the cash value is sufficient to pay premiums.
QID: 1259

34.   C.   Under a participating whole life policy, if an individual needs more life insurance, he or she can use dividends to buy paid-up additions.
QID: 1260

35.   C.   There are five common dividend options taking dividends in cash, applying dividends against premium payments, leaving dividends with the company to accumulate at interest, buying paid-up additions and buying one-year term protection.
QID: 1261

36.   C.   Policy dividends are not taxable income because they are considered a partial return of premiums paid.
QID: 1262

37.   B.   Of the five common dividend options, leaving dividends with the company to accumulate at interest is the only choice that directly produces interest income.
QID: 1263

38.   B.   Policy dividends, issued on participating policies (policies in which the insureds may participate in the operating and investment results of the insurer), are a reflection of favorable operations, investment or mortality results. They are never guaranteed. In fact, most states require life insurance proposals that contain dividend illustrations to state that future dividends are not guaranteed.
QID: 1264

39. A. Under the cash refund option, the company will pay the difference between the original proceeds ($50,000) and the total payments made to the primary beneficiary ($21,300). That amount is paid to the secondary beneficiary in a lump sum.
QID: 1278

40. A. Under the interest-only option, only the interest on the face amount will be paid to the wife on a regular basis. The face amount ($85,000) will be saved for the children.
QID: 1279

41. C. Under a settlement option, the relationship created between the beneficiary and insurance company is that of creditor and debtor since the insurance company is obligated to fulfill the terms of the settlement.
QID: 1280

42. D. The life income option provides that income payments will continue as long as the primary beneficiary lives and even if the principal is depleted.
QID: 1281

43. A. Under a fixed-period life insurance settlement option, excess interest will increase the size of payments. Insurers may choose to pay interest over and above the guaranteed rate if they have sufficiently high earnings.
QID: 1282

44. C. Under a fixed-amount settlement option, selection of a smaller payment will increase the payment periods. Interest rates do not affect the payment amount on a fixed-amount option. Instead, they affect the length of the payment period. If there is excess interest to be paid, it will lengthen the payment period rather than the amount of the payment.
QID: 1283

45. C. Under an installment refund option, if the primary beneficiary dies, installments of the same amount continue to the secondary beneficiary until all installments paid to both beneficia-

ries equal the original amount of proceeds. Under a life income-only option, installments are paid to the primary beneficiary as long as he or she lives, with no return of principal guaranteed. Therefore, this option provides the largest installments per $1,000 of proceeds. The lump sum option is not used as extensively today as other options.
QID: 1284

46. B. Under an installment refund option, the same income payments continue to the secondary beneficiary after the primary beneficiary dies, until the entire death benefit amount is paid.
QID: 1285

47. B. Under an installment refund settlement option, if the primary beneficiary dies, the secondary beneficiary will receive the same income payments until the total amount paid out to both beneficiaries equals the original amount of proceeds.
QID: 1286

48. A. Under a period-certain income option, installments are payable for the duration of that period, whether or not the primary beneficiary lives. In this case, installments are payable for a period of 10 years. Since the primary beneficiary died after six years, the secondary beneficiary will be paid the same installments for four more years.
QID: 1287

49. C. The shorter the period certain, the higher the monthly payment rate.
QID: 1288

50. B. The fact that the policy's proceeds $250,000 were available for distribution upon the wife's death indicates that they had been held and that she received interest payments.
QID: 1289

51. D. The joint and one-half survivor life income option provides an income for two people. In this case, the couple, while both are living, gets the full amount; the survivor, half the amount, or $225.
QID: 1290

52.   D.   The joint and two-thirds survivor life income option provides an income for two people the full amount for the couple, while both are living; two-thirds of the amount for the survivor.
QID: 1291

53.   C.   Group insurance involves experience rating, which is a method of establishing a premium for the group based on the group's previous claims experience.
QID: 1295

54.   B.   Generally, premiums paid for personal life insurance policies by individual policyowners are considered to be personal expenses and are not deductible from gross income. Premiums paid for business life insurance usually are also not deductible. However, premiums paid for life insurance owned by a qualified charitable organization are deductible.
QID: 3317

55.   A.   Three primary factors are considered when computing the basic premium for life insurance mortality, interest and expense. Of these, the mortality factor has the greatest effect on premium calculations. That is, while an insurer's interest and expense factors are generally the same for all of its policyowners, the mortality factor can vary greatly, depending on the personal characteristics of individual insureds.
QID: 3318

7

Life Insurance Policy Provisions

1. The insured in a $25,000 life insurance policy died of a heart attack. Since the policy had a "double indemnity" provision, the policy beneficiary received

   A. nothing
   B. $12,500
   C. $25,000
   D. $50,000

2. Which of the following options is designed to protect the policyowner should the policy be in danger of lapsing for nonpayment of premium?

   A. waiver of premium
   B. guaranteed insurability
   C. premium exclusion
   D. automatic premium loan

3. Lisa exercised her automatic premium loan provision to pay her annual premium on her $50,000 life insurance policy. She died four months after the loan was taken, never having a chance to repay it. Given these facts, which of the following is CORRECT?

   A. The premium was paid by the insurance company from its reserves.
   B. The amount paid to Lisa's beneficiary as the death proceeds was reduced by the amount of the loan.
   C. The policy was canceled, since the loan was not repaid.
   D. The type of insurance Lisa owned was term.

4. Which provision of a life insurance policy declares that the application is part of the contract?

   A. Insuring clause
   B. Ownership clause
   C. Entire contract clause
   D. Incontestable clause

5. Which of the following statements is CORRECT?

   A. If an insuring company revises its bylaws or practices, any life insurance contract issued prior to the change must be modified to reflect the company's new policies.
   B. After a policy is delivered to and accepted by the policyowner, it cannot be changed in any way, except in accordance with terms stated in the contract.
   C. If a premium deposit is not paid with the application, the policy will still be valid if the applicant is acceptable to the insurer's underwriters.
   D. Misrepresentations made in an application are always considered grounds for voiding an insurance contract.

6. All of the following statements pertaining to the insuring clause in a life insurance policy are correct EXCEPT

   A. it specifies how much the company will pay and when payment will be made
   B. it is usually the first clause in a life insurance policy
   C. it names the insured
   D. it gives the policyowners the right to return the policy if not satisfied

7. "Further, the Company agrees to pay the surrender value to the owner if the insured is alive on the maturity date." This is an example of a(n)

   A. consideration clause
   B. insuring clause
   C. surrender clause
   D. entire contract clause

8. All of the following statements pertaining to the incontestable clause in a life insurance policy are correct EXCEPT

   A. the clause applies to all policy provisions, including accidental death riders
   B. it gives reassurance to the policyowner
   C. if the insured lives beyond the incontestable period, the company cannot later contest the policy for misrepresentation so long as the premiums are paid
   D. the specified period after which an insurer cannot contest a policy is usually two years after policy issue

9. Which of the following is a circumstance in which the incontestable clause of an insurance policy would apply?

   A. impersonation of the applicant by another
   B. no insurable interest
   C. intent to murder
   D. concealment of smoking

10. All of the following statements pertaining to the suicide clause in a life insurance policy are correct EXCEPT

    A. The insured with a $75,000 life insurance policy issued December 15, 1997, committed suicide December 24, 1999. The beneficiary of the policy received a return of the premiums paid for the policy.
    B. The suicide clause is designed to protect the insuring company.
    C. An insured committed suicide on February 1, 1999. The insured had a $50,000 life insurance policy issued January 28, 1997. The $50,000 death benefit was paid to the beneficiary of the policy.
    D. The suicide clause stipulates a period of time during which benefits will not be paid if the insured commits suicide.

11. Vivian commits suicide four years after taking out a $100,000 life insurance policy on herself. Her beneficiary is concerned that the death claim will be denied. In this case, all of the following are correct statements EXCEPT

    A. the suicide clause in Vivian's policy would have expired, so it would not affect the death claim
    B. the company has definite proof of the cause of her death, so it can refuse to pay the death benefit
    C. if the suicide clause were in effect, the company would refund the premiums paid
    D. if the beneficiary were familiar with the policy's suicide clause, he or she would not doubt payment of the claim

12. Which of the following is stated in the consideration clause of a life insurance policy?

    A. Age of the insured
    B. Insured's general physical condition
    C. Policyowner's occupational classification
    D. Amount and frequency of premium payments

13. Joshua returns to the agent the new life insurance policy delivered by the agent three days earlier. Joshua had paid the initial premium. Assuming his policy has a "free-look" provision, what is Joshua entitled to receive?

    A. The policy's cash surrender value
    B. A partial refund of the initial premium
    C. A credit that can be applied to the purchase of another policy
    D. A full refund of the initial premium

14. Janet, the insured, dies during a grace period for her $50,000 life policy. What happens, considering that her premium has not been paid?

    A. The premium is canceled because the insured died during the grace period.
    B. The amount of the premium due is deducted from the policy proceeds paid to the beneficiary.
    C. The premium due, plus a 10 percent penalty, is charged against the policy.
    D. The beneficiary must pay the premium after the death claim is paid.

15. Which of the following provisions of a life insurance contract generally helps to keep policies in force if policyowners neglect to pay their premiums?

    A. Grace period
    B. Insuring clause
    C. Free-look period
    D. Incontestable clause

16. Edna stopped paying premiums on her permanent life insurance policy seven years ago though she never surrendered it. She is still insurable and has no outstanding loan against the policy. The company probably will decline to reinstate the policy because the time limit for reinstatement has expired. The limit usually is

    A. 60 to 90 days
    B. 6 months to 18 months
    C. One year
    D. Three or five years

17. All of the following statements pertaining to reinstating a life insurance policy are correct EXCEPT

    A. all back premiums must be paid
    B. any outstanding policy loan must be repaid
    C. the insured must provide evidence of insurability
    D. the cash surrender value must be forfeited to the insurer

18. All of the following statements pertaining to reinstatement of a life insurance policy are correct EXCEPT

   A. a suicide exclusion period is renewed with a reinstated policy
   B. when reinstating a policy, the company must charge the policyowner for past-due premiums
   C. when reinstating a policy, the company must charge the policyowner for interest on past-due premiums
   D. a new contestable period becomes effective in a reinstated policy

19. All of the following are rights of policy ownership EXCEPT

   A. selecting a settlement option
   B. changing a policy provision with the agent's approval
   C. selecting a nonforfeiture option
   D. designating beneficiaries

20. All of the following are life insurance policyowner's rights EXCEPT the right to

   A. name a beneficiary irrevocably
   B. change the mode of premium payment
   C. change the grace period
   D. take a policy loan

21. All of the following statements pertaining to life policy assignment are correct EXCEPT

   A. to secure a loan, the policy temporarily can be transferred to the lender as security for the loan
   B. the policyowner must obtain approval from the insurance company before a policy can be assigned
   C. the life insurance company assumes no responsibility for the validity of an assignment
   D. the policyowner must notify the company, in writing, of any assignment

22. Alexandria assigns one of her $10,000 life insurance policies to a bank as collateral for a loan. The assignee is

   A. Alexandria, the insured
   B. the bank
   C. the beneficiary of the policy
   D. the insurance company

23. An assignment in which the assignee receives full control over the policy is called a(n)

   A. collateral assignment
   B. absolute assignment
   C. guaranteed assignment
   D. revocable assignment

24. Which of the following statements pertaining to the misstatement of age provision of a life insurance policy is CORRECT?

   A. If a deceased insured under a $30,000 life insurance policy is found to be younger than the policy showed, the insured's beneficiary will receive $30,000 if the policy's incontestable clause has expired.
   B. The beneficiary of a policy with a $45,000 face amount will receive more than $45,000 if it is found that the deceased insured was older than the policy indicated, and if the policy's incontestable clause has expired.
   C. If an insurer discovers that a policyowner has misstated his or her age on the policy application, the policy becomes void and the beneficiary will receive nothing.
   D. The insurer discovers that a deceased policyowner had lied about her age on a $75,000 life insurance policy. The insurer will pay her beneficiary what her premiums would have purchased if she had given her age truthfully.

25. Abner's age was misstated in his application for a $50,000 life policy. What will the company do when it discovers the error?

    A. The company will amend the application, but no additional premium can be charged.
    B. It probably will void the policy.
    C. It will adjust either the premium rate or the amount of protection.
    D. It will do nothing because the policy cannot be altered in any way after it has been issued.

26. Which of the following policyowner rights relates directly to the cash value of permanent insurance?

    A. Right to change premium mode
    B. Right to assign proceeds
    C. Right to name beneficiaries
    D. Right to take a policy loan

27. Roberta is the insured in a $30,000 life insurance policy for which she pays an annual premium of $700. There is an outstanding policy loan of $2,500. Her last premium due has not been paid and she dies during the grace period. How much will her beneficiary receive?

    A. $26,800
    B. $27,500
    C. $29,300
    D. $30,000

28. Typically excluded from coverage in a life insurance policy would be death from any of the following causes EXCEPT

    A. hazardous occupation
    B. hazardous hobby
    C. war
    D. commercial aviation

29. An insurer received a request on March 1, 2000, for payment of a policy's full cash surrender value. Under the laws of most states, the insurer could delay payment until

    A. September 1, 2000
    B. December 1, 2000
    C. March 1, 2001
    D. June 1, 2001

30. The "delayed payment" provision in a whole life policy provides that the

    A. insured may postpone premium payment if he or she can demonstrate cause
    B. insured may postpone his or her initial premium payment for 30 days
    C. insurance company may delay payment of the cash surrender value for six months after the policyowner's request for payment
    D. insurance company may delay paying the policy proceeds to the beneficiary for 90 days

31. Roland purchases a life insurance policy and names his wife, Carol, as beneficiary. Roland's children, Sue and Bob, are to share the benefits equally if she dies before him. His church is to receive the proceeds if his wife and children all predecease him. The primary beneficiary is

    A. Carol
    B. Sue
    C. Bob
    D. the church

32. Roland buys a life insurance policy and names his wife, Carol, as beneficiary. Roland's children, Bob and Sue, are to share the benefits equally if Carol dies before him. His church is to receive the proceeds if his wife and children predecease him. How would the proceeds of Roland's policy be distributed if both his children predecease him?

   A. Carol would receive 50 percent of the proceeds.
   B. Carol would receive 75 percent of the proceeds.
   C. The church would receive 100 percent of the proceeds.
   D. Carol would receive 100 percent of the proceeds.

33. If a beneficiary has been so designated that he or she acquires a vested right in the policy immediately upon its issuance, the designation is termed

   A. vested
   B. contractual
   C. irrevocable
   D. primary

34. All of the following statements pertaining to beneficiaries of life insurance policies are correct EXCEPT

   A. A widower dies with two sons as beneficiaries in his life policy. One son died previously, leaving two children who are to share in their father's portion of the proceeds. This is a per stirpes beneficiary arrangement.
   B. A widow dies with two daughters as beneficiaries to her life policy. One daughter died previously, leaving the other daughter as sole beneficiary to receive the proceeds. This is a per capita beneficiary arrangement.
   C. Named beneficiaries must be individuals, not organizations or businesses.
   D. A widower dies and leaves his estate to "My Children" without naming them individually. This kind of beneficiary is known as a class designation.

35. Assume Clarence, the insured, designated his estate as the beneficiary of his life insurance policy. Based on that, which of the following statements is CORRECT?

   A. The amount of Clarence's estate will be reduced by the amount of proceeds it receives.
   B. The heirs will be able to select specific settlement options from the estate, just as if they were the direct beneficiaries.
   C. Clarence's creditors can attach the proceeds more readily than if the proceeds were paid to named beneficiaries.
   D. The proceeds will not be included in Clarence's gross estate for estate tax purposes.

36. The beneficiary on Susan's life insurance policy reads, "Children of the Insured." Which of the following phrases BEST describes this type of beneficiary designation?

    A. Juvenile beneficiaries
    B. Class beneficiaries
    C. Generational beneficiaries
    D. Basic beneficiaries

37. Which of the following terms indicates the insured's right to change beneficiaries in a life insurance

    A. Per stirpes
    B. Revocable
    C. Per capita
    D. Irrevocable

38. Ted, the insured in a $75,000 life policy, and his sole beneficiary, Maxine, are killed instantly when their car is struck by a train. Under the Uniform Simultaneous Death Act, to whose estate will the policy proceeds be payable?

    A. Maxine's estate
    B. Ted's estate
    C. Both Ted's and Maxine's estates, equally
    D. The proceeds will escheat to the state

39. Under a common disaster clause in a life insurance policy, it is assumed that the

    A. insured died last, unless the primary beneficiary lives beyond a stipulated period
    B. contingent beneficiary is entitled to the policy proceeds
    C. primary beneficiary died last, unless the insured lives beyond a stipulated period
    D. insured and primary beneficiary died simultaneously

40. Winston, the insured, and his wife, Irene, his sole beneficiary, both died in a hotel fire. Hospital physicians witnessed that Irene lived at least two hours longer than Winston. The life policy had no common disaster clause. Which of the following will likely receive the policy proceeds?

    A. Irene's estate
    B. Winston's secondary beneficiary
    C. Winston's estate
    D. The state

41. A spendthrift clause in a life insurance policy is designed to protect the

    A. insured
    B. insurance company
    C. insured's creditors
    D. insured's beneficiary

42. All of the following statements pertaining to the spendthrift clause in a life insurance policy are correct EXCEPT

    A. It is designed to protect beneficiaries against the claims of creditors.
    B. It does not exempt proceeds paid to beneficiaries in a lump sum.
    C. A beneficiary receives $125 per month from a life policy under the fixed-amount settlement option and a spendthrift clause. The beneficiary may have the company send the payments to a creditor to pay off a debt.
    D. The exemption applies only to money held in trust by the insurance company that is payable at some future time to the named beneficiary.

43. All of the following policyowner rights contribute to the flexibility of a life insurance policy EXCEPT

    A. Settlement options
    B. Nonforfeiture options
    C. Classification of the applicant
    D. Beneficiary selection

44. All of the following statements pertaining to the conversion privilege of group term life insurance are correct EXCEPT

    A. an insured employee typically has 31 days following termination of employment in which to convert the group insurance
    B. when a group plan is terminated, group coverage of the insureds generally is extended for 60 days
    C. insureds who convert their coverage to individual policies pay a premium rate according to their attained age
    D. a covered individual may exercise the conversion privilege regardless of his or her insurability

45. When a life insurance beneficiary is revocable,

    A. the policyowner may change the beneficiary only with the beneficiary's consent
    B. the beneficiary has no vested claims in the policy or its proceeds while the insured is living
    C. the policyowner is limited with respect to how many times he or she can change the beneficiary during the policy's term
    D. the policyowner and the beneficiary share ownership of the policy

46. Which of the following statements about viatical settlements is CORRECT?

    A. The viatical company generally pays the insured 30 to 60 percent of the policy's face value.
    B. The insured receives part of the death benefit when the policy is sold and the rest at death.
    C. Proceeds are exempt from federal income tax.
    D. The insured must continue paying premiums after the viatical settlement is completed.

47. Which of the following statements about portable group term life insurance i CORRECT?

    A. An employee can convert a term policy to a whole life policy.
    B. The premium rates are lower than individually sold coverage.
    C. The term policy builds cash values, unlike individual term life insurance.
    D. The premium rates decrease every year.

48. Which provision sets forth the insurer's basic promise to pay benefits upon the insured's death?

    A. Consideration clause
    B. Reinstatement provision
    C. Settlement options provision
    D. Insuring clause

49. All of the following statements about accelerated benefits provisions are correct EXCEPT

    A. They are now standard in life insurance policies.
    B. The death benefit, less the accelerated payment, is still payable.
    C. The money received as an accelerated benefit must be used to pay medical expenses.
    D. They provide for the early payment of part of a policy's face amount if the insured suffers from a terminal illness or injury.

50. The most common approach used today to distribute life insurance policy proceeds to a person's descendants is

    A. per stirpes
    B. revocable
    C. per capita
    D. irrevocable

51. The most common method used today for changing beneficiaries is called the

    A. assignment method
    B. reversionary method
    C. recording method
    D. beneficiary alteration method

52. Which clause in a life insurance policy protects beneficiaries from the claims of their creditors?

    A. Facility-of-payment provision
    B. Spendthrift trust clause
    C. Per capita clause
    D. Debtor provision

Answers & Rationale

1. C. Under a "double indemnity" provision, the policy beneficiary would receive double the face amount in the event of a fatal accidental injury. Since the insured's death was not due to an accident, the policy paid its $25,000 face amount.
QID: 1189

2. D. Under the automatic premium loan provision, the cash values will be used to pay the premium if the premium due has not been paid by the end of the grace period.
QID: 1191

3. B. The policyowner's cash values are used to pay premium loans. If the loan is not repaid at the time of the insured's death, the amount plus interest is subtracted from the death proceeds.
QID: 1192

4. C. The entire contract clause states that the entire contract consists of the policy and an attached copy of the application, including a report of the insured's physical condition.
QID: 1228

5. B. Because of the entire contract provision, policyowners are protected against arbitrary changes by the issuing company. Issued policies are not affected by later changes of any kind in an insurer's bylaws or practices. The policy can only be changed in accordance with terms spelled out in the contract. Applications for policies must be accompanied by the initial premium, or a portion of it. Misrepresentations are considered fraudulent and grounds for voiding a contract if they are material to the risk and are made with the intent to defraud.
QID: 1229

6. D. The insuring clause is the company's promise to pay. The "free-look" provision allows the insured to return the policy within a specified time, if not satisfied.
QID: 1230

7. B. The insuring clause defines and describes the scope of coverage provided and limits of indemnification. Keep in mind that the clause is not actually titled as such, but it appears on the cover of the policy.
QID: 1231

8. A. The incontestable clause applies to death benefits only. It generally does not apply to any rider that provides accidental death or disability benefits.
QID: 1232

9. D. After a policy has been in force for the specified term, the insurer cannot contest a death claim or refuse payment of proceeds for a concealment of smoking. A policy issued under one of the other three situations may be voided at any time, since it would not be considered a valid, enforceable contract.
QID: 1233

10. A. Suicide clauses typically extend two years, during which time the insurer will not have to pay benefits if the insured does, in fact, commit suicide. The insuring company is obligated to return the premiums paid. In this situation, the insured committed suicide nine days after the clause time period expired; therefore, the insurer must pay the benefits to the beneficiary.
QID: 1234

11. B. As a general practice, the suicide clause provides that death benefits are payable in full after the policy has been in force for two years, even if the insured did commit suicide.
QID: 1235

12. D. The consideration clause of a life insurance policy states the amount and frequency of premium payments on a separate schedule within the policy.
QID: 1236

13. D.   Under the "free look" provision, policyowners have either 10 or 20 days to examine their new life policies. If not satisfied with the policy, a policyowner may return it to the insurer and receive a full refund of the initial payment.
QID: 1237

14. B.   If an insured dies during the grace period of a life policy, the amount of the premium due is deducted from the policy proceeds paid to the beneficiary.
QID: 1238

15. A.   The grace period provides additional time—usually 30 days after the premium due date—in which the policyowner can pay the premium. The insuring clause describes the terms that define the insurance contract. The free-look provision gives the insured a time period to examine the policy and return it for a full refund of the first premium if dissatisfied for any reason. The incontestable clause provides that after a certain amount of time, the insurer no longer has the right to contest the validity of the policy.
QID: 1239

16. D.   The policyowner has only a limited period of time (typically three or five years) after discontinuing premiums in which to reinstate a lapsed policy.
QID: 1240

17. D.   Paying back premiums and any policy loans, as well as proving insurability, are required before a lapsed policy will be reinstated. The policyowner does not forfeit his or her cash values.
QID: 1241

18. A.   When reinstating a life policy, no new suicide exclusion period goes into effect.
QID: 1242

19. B.   Owning a life insurance policy provides certain rights and choices. However, changing a policy provision with or without the agent's approval is not one of them.
QID: 1243

20. C.   The policyowner has no right to change the grace period. That provision is a contractual clause developed by the insurer according to individual state laws.
QID: 1244

21. B.   A policyowner may "assign" or transfer ownership of a life policy to anyone without the insurer's approval.
QID: 1245

22. B.   When a life insurance policy is assigned, the recipient of the policy (in this case, the bank) is called the "assignee."
QID: 1246

23. B.   Under an absolute assignment, the transfer is complete and irrevocable. A collateral assignment is one in which the policy is assigned to a creditor as security for a debt until the debt is satisfied.
QID: 1247

24. D.   Situations in which the insured's age is in error are covered under the "misstatement of age" provision. This provision states that the policy's benefit will be equal to what the premium the insured did pay would have purchased if the age were correct. Thus, the benefit payable is adjusted up or down in proportion to what the premium that was paid bears to the premium which should have been paid. The incontestable clause has no bearing on a misstatement of age.
QID: 1248

25. C.   Because Abner's age was misstated in his application, the company will adjust either the premium rate or the amount of the protection.
QID: 1249

26. D.   A policyowner has the right to take a policy loan based on the cash value buildup in his or her policy.
QID: 1250

27. A.   When a death claim is filed against a life policy, all amounts due on that policy are subtracted from the death benefit. This includes any policy loans, plus interest due, and any outstand-

ing premiums. In this case, $30,000 minus $700 (annual premium owed) minus $2,500 (outstanding policy loan) equals $26,800.
QID: 1251

28. D. A life policy might exclude death due to piloting an aircraft (a hazardous hobby or occupation), but it typically would not exclude death by a commercial airplane accident.
QID: 1252

29. A. Laws in most states permit insurers to postpone payment for a policy's full cash surrender value for six months.
QID: 1253

30. C. While rarely used, the delayed payment provision enables the insurer to postpone payment of the cash surrender value for six months after the policyowner requests payment.
QID: 1254

31. A. When an insured dies, the first person in line to receive the death proceeds is the primary beneficiary.
QID: 1265

32. D. In this case, the church as tertiary (third) beneficiary would receive proceeds only if and when all primary and secondary beneficiaries predecease the insured. As Carol is the primary beneficiary, she would receive 100 percent of the proceeds.
QID: 1266

33. C. If a beneficiary is named irrevocably, the policyowner has given up his or her right to change that beneficiary and, unless otherwise specified in the policy, the owner cannot take any action that would affect the right of that beneficiary to receive the full amount of the insurance at the insured's death. This includes taking out a policy loan or surrendering the policy.
QID: 1267

34. C. "Per stirpes" and "per capita" are terms meaning, respectively, "by the branch" and "by the person." A per stirpes designation provides that proceeds are to split in such a way that the

share of any deceased beneficiary will go to that person's surviving children. A per capital designation provides that proceeds are to be shared on a named basis; if any named beneficiary predeceases the insured, his or her share will be split evenly among the surviving named beneficiaries. Businesses, trusts, charitable organizations and other estates are all acceptable beneficiaries.
QID: 1268

35. C. If insurance proceeds are paid directly to an insured's estate, the size of the estate will be increased by the amount of the proceeds. Settlement options will be lost to heirs, since an estate will distribute its assets in lump sums. Creditors can attach proceeds more readily if they are paid to an estate. The value of the policy will be included in the gross estate for tax purposes.
QID: 1269

36. B. A policyowner may designate a group of beneficiaries without specifying one or more of the beneficiaries by name, through use of the phrase "class beneficiaries."
QID: 1270

37. B. "Revocable" is a term indicating the insured's right to change beneficiaries in a life insurance policy.
QID: 1271

38. B. The Uniform Simultaneous Death Act provides that, if the insured and primary beneficiary are killed in the same accident and there is not sufficient evidence to show who died first, the policy proceeds are to be distributed as if the insured died last. Ted's estate would receive the proceeds, since Maxine, the beneficiary, was deemed to have predeceased Ted, and no other beneficiary was named.
QID: 1272

39. A. Under a common disaster clause in a life insurance policy, it is assumed that the insured died last, unless the primary beneficiary lives beyond a stipulated period (usually 14 or 30 days). If the primary beneficiary does not live

beyond that period, proceeds are payable to the insured's secondary beneficiary or to his or her estate.
QID: 1273

40. A.   In light of the witnesses to the deaths in this problem and in the absence of the common disaster clause, Irene's estate should receive the proceeds. She, as primary beneficiary, outlived the insured
QID: 1274

41. D.   The spendthrift clause in a life insurance policy is designed to protect beneficiaries from the claims of their creditors.
QID: 1275

42. C.   The spendthrift clause in a life insurance policy is designed to protect beneficiaries from their creditors by providing that the death benefits payable are not subject to creditor claims. This clause applies only while the insurer holds the money, and only to installment payments.
QID: 1276

43. C.   Nonforfeiture options provide help when the insured no longer wants to pay premiums. Settlement options offer a choice of ways in which proceeds can be paid. Choosing and changing the beneficiary is a right of the policyowner. Classifying the applicant according to his or her risk is the right of the insurer.
QID: 1277

44. B.   When a group plan is terminated, group coverage of the insureds generally is extended for 31 days.
QID: 1292

45. B.   When beneficiaries are revocable, the policyowner may change beneficiaries at any time. The policyowner also retains complete ownership of the policy, and may change the beneficiary any number of times during the term's policy. A revocable beneficiary has no vested claim in the policy or its proceeds while the insured is living.
QID: 3319

46. C.   Through viatical settlements, individuals who are terminally or chronically ill sell their life insurance policies to viatical companies for 50 to 80 percent of the policy's face value. The viatical company becomes the policyowner and is responsible for paying premiums. When the insured dies, the company receives the death benefit. The proceeds paid to a terminally or chronically ill individual are exempt from federal income tax.
QID: 3320

47. B.   Many employers now offer portable group term life insurance, which means that employees can take or "port" their insurance with them. The insurance coverage remains a term life benefit with no cash value. All of the ported policies are pooled together rather than remaining in the employer's plan. The rates are therefore more like group rates and are much lower than individually sold coverage.
QID: 3321

48. D.   The insuring clause sets forth the insurer's basic promise to pay benefits upon the insured's death. It is usually found on the first page of the policy and identifies the parties to the contract.
QID: 3322

49. C.   Accelerated benefits provisions are standard in life insurance policies. They provide for the early payment of part of a policy's face amount if the insured suffers from a terminal illness or injury. The death benefit, less the accelerated payment, is still payable. The insured may spend the money received as he or she wishes. It does not have to be spent on final expenses or medical expenses.
QID: 3323

50. A.   The *per stirpes* method of distribution is by far the more common approach that is used to distribute life insurance policy proceeds to a person's descendants. A per stirpes distribution means that a beneficiary's share of a policy's pro-

ceeds will be passed on down to his or her living child or children in equal shares if he or she (the named beneficiary) predeceases the insured.
QID: 3324

51. C. The most common method used today to change beneficiaries is called the recording method. Under this method, the policyowner notifies the insurance company in writing of the beneficiary change. When the insurer records the change, it becomes effective as of the date the insured signed the notice.
QID: 3325

52. B. A spendthrift trust clause is used to help protect beneficiaries from the claims of their creditors. It shelters life insurance proceeds that have not yet been paid to a named beneficiary from the claims of either the beneficiary's or policyowner's creditors.
QID: 3326

8

Annuities

1. All of the following statements regarding annuities are correct EXCEPT

   A. an annuity contract provides for the purchase of income
   B. an annuity is based on mortality assumptions and the law of large numbers
   C. annuity payments are guaranteed
   D. like life insurance, an annuity is used primarily to provide income at death

2. A principal function of annuities is to

   A. create an estate
   B. provide for surviving dependents
   C. liquidate an estate
   D. reduce income taxes

3. Annuities are classified by all of the following EXCEPT

   A. method of payment (single vs. periodic)
   B. number of lives covered (single vs. joint)
   C. disposition of proceeds (fixed vs. variable)
   D. who issues them

4. Typically, how frequently are annuity payments distributed to the annuitant?

   A. Weekly
   B. Monthly
   C. Semi-annually
   D. Annually

5. All of the following are factors that determine the annuity benefit amount EXCEPT

   A. Annuitant's age
   B. Annuitant's sex
   C. Company's expense (loading) factor
   D. Annuitant's tax bracket

6. The time during which funds are being paid into an annuity is called the

   A. annuity period
   B. accumulation period
   C. savings period
   D. paid-up period

7. All of the following are annuity premium factors EXCEPT

   A. medical history
   B. age
   C. sex
   D. assumed interest rate

8. If both an older and younger person had annuity funds of the same amount and simultaneously began to receive monthly life payments, which individual would receive the LARGER payments?

   A. Older person
   B. Younger person
   C. Both would receive the same amount.
   D. The amount of the payment is based on the purchase date of the annuity.

9. If all other factors are equal, which assumed interest rate results in a LOWER cost to a variable annuity owner?

   A. Lower
   B. Higher
   C. Level
   D. Average

10. The loading factor in annuities takes into consideration all of the following EXCEPT

    A. agents' commissions
    B. clerical support
    C. general cost of doing business
    D. annuitant's age

11. All of the following statements regarding annuities are correct EXCEPT

    A. Pure life annuities provide income as long as the annuitant lives; benefits terminate at his or her death.
    B. An installment refund annuity guarantees a specific amount of benefits, payable to the annuitant only; if death occurs prior to total payout, a portion of the premium is refunded to the annuitant's estate or beneficiary.
    C. Annuities that pay benefits in specified dollar amounts are fixed annuities; annuities that pay benefits in relation to units are variable annuities.
    D. An annuity can be classified as "immediate" or "deferred," depending on when benefit payments begin.

12. The annuitant of an annuity can be compared to which of the following with respect to a life insurance policy?

    A. Insured
    B. Policyowner
    C. Beneficiary
    D. Creditor

13. Which of the following individuals has made the BEST use of an annuity?

    A. Brian would like to protect his wife and son against the contingency of his premature death and also supplement future retirement income. He therefore purchases an annuity rather than a life insurance contract.
    B. Mary wants to be sure that she has enough cash on hand in case she is temporarily out of work. She buys an annuity with the idea that she can cash it in if she becomes unemployed and needs the money while she looks for another job.
    C. Sue wants to be sure that her children have enough income to pay for college in the event she dies. To provide funds for her children's education, she buys an annuity.
    D. Tony wants to be sure that he has enough income after he retires. To adequately provide for himself and his wife after he stops working, he buys an annuity now.

14. All of the following statements pertaining to an immediate annuity are correct EXCEPT

    A. An immediate annuity is funded with a single payment.
    B. An immediate annuity has a long accumulation period.
    C. An immediate annuity is designed to make its first benefit payment to the annuitant at the first payment from the date of purchase.
    D. An immediate annuity usually makes its first payment one month from the purchase date.

15. A variable annuity guarantees which of the following?

    A. The amount of the annuity benefit payments
    B. The rate of return credited to the annuity fund
    C. The value of the amount of the annuity over the life of the accumulation period
    D. The investment involves a risk

16. What type of annuity payment option provides a guaranteed income to the annuitant for life and, if the annuitant dies before the annuity is depleted, a lump-sum cash payment to the annuitant's beneficiary?

    A. Period certain option
    B. Straight life option
    C. Installment refund option
    D. Cash refund option

17. Annuities may be purchased with all of the following EXCEPT

    A. single lump-sum payment
    B. schedule of fixed payments
    C. schedule of flexible payments
    D. a single payment that may be deferred for five years

18. If an annuitant has a refund annuity and dies after the annuity income begins, his or her beneficiary will receive

    A. nothing
    B. a predetermined lump-sum cash payment
    C. a lump-sum cash payment equal to the starting annuity fund
    D. a lump-sum cash payment equal to the starting annuity fund, less the amount of income already paid the deceased

19. Fred, age 60, has three years until he retires. He decides to surrender his whole life insurance policy and use the cash value to fund a single premium annuity. How many payments will he make to fund the annuity?

    A. One
    B. Three
    C. Seven
    D. As many as he wishes

20. Rick purchased an annuity, making a single lump-sum payment on September 1, 2000. His benefits began on October 1, 2000. What kind of annuity did Rick buy?

    A. Immediate
    B. Deferred
    C. Secondary
    D. Continual

21. What annuity payout option provides for lifetime payments to the annuitant but guarantees a certain minimum term of payments, whether or not the annuitant is living?

    A. Installment refund option
    B. Life with period certain
    C. Period certain
    D. Straight life income

22. What type of annuity settlement arrangement stops making payments when the annuitant dies?

    A. Pure life annuity
    B. Cash refund annuity
    C. Installment refund annuity
    D. Period certain annuity

23. James died after receiving $180 monthly for six years from a $25,000 installment refund annuity. His wife Lucy, as beneficiary, now will receive the same monthly income until her payments total

    A. $2,160
    B. $12,040
    C. $12,960
    D. $25,000

24. Which annuity settlement arrangement guarantees to pay at least a minimum amount equal to the original investment?

A. Joint and full survivor annuity
B. Period certain annuity
C. Installment refund annuity
D. Pure life annuity

25. Which of the following types of annuity payout options guarantees as a minimum the payout of the entire annuity principal amount?

A. Cash refund
B. Pure life
C. Period certain
D. Joint and full survivor option

26. Which of the following statements pertaining to annuity settlement arrangements is CORRECT?

A. The survivor under a joint and full survivor annuity receives 100 percent of the original joint income.
B. An installment refund annuity provides that, when the original annuitant dies, the same income will continue to the beneficiary until the beneficiary dies.
C. The survivor under a joint and full survivor annuity receives 50 percent of the original income.
D. A straight life income pays whatever is left in the annuity to the annuitant's beneficiary if the annuitant dies.

27. All of the following statements pertaining to variable annuities are correct EXCEPT

A. the rate of growth is variable
B. the payments to the annuitants are variable
C. if the net contribution to a variable annuity account is $350 and the cost of one accumulation unit is $87.50, three units would be assigned to that account
D. during the accumulation period, the number of accumulation units in the account will continue to grow

28. During the accumulation period of a deferred variable annuity, the value of the individual account rises or falls based on the

A. variable premiums
B. number of annuitants
C. investment results
D. insurer's expenses

29. Mark's variable annuity currently has 2,500 accumulation units. If each unit is valued at $3.00, the total dollar value of his account is

A. $833
B. $2,500
C. $7,500
D. $8,330

30. Nonqualified annuity benefits are a combination of principal and interest. As such, what is the tax status of the portion of the benefit payments that represents a return of principal?

A. Taxable when received
B. Not taxable
C. Tax-deferred until death
D. Added to the face amount and taxed when received

31. Employees of which of the following generally may participate in a tax-sheltered annuity (TSA) plan?

A. Public school systems
B. Professional sports teams
C. Professional partnerships
D. Manufacturing plants

32. Which of the following statements pertaining to tax-sheltered annuities (TSAs) is CORRECT?

    A. TSAs are available to any worker not covered by an employer-sponsored retirement plan.
    B. TSAs are available to employees of certain nonprofit organizations.
    C. Fred, a schoolteacher participating in a tax-deferred annuity, will receive his benefits tax-free.
    D. Alice, a vice-president of a computer software company, can invest in a tax-sheltered annuity.

33. Annuity payments are taxable to the extent that they represent interest earned rather than capital returned. What method is used to determine the taxable portion of each payment?

    A. Exclusion ratio
    B. Marginal tax formula
    C. Surtax ratio
    D. Annuitization ratio

34. When a cash value life insurance policy is converted into an annuity in a nontaxable transaction, the event is generally known as a

    A. rollover
    B. 1035 exchange
    C. modified endowment
    D. pension enhancement

35. All of the following statements about immediate annuities are correct EXCEPT

    A. The income flow must be fixed rather than variable.
    B. They have relatively short accumulation periods.
    C. They can only be funded with a single payment.
    D. The first benefit payment is typically made one month from the purchase date.

36. Which of the following statements about an equity indexed annuity is CORRECT?

    A. It is very similar to a variable annuity.
    B. It can decrease in value.
    C. It does not have a fixed minimum guarantee.
    D. It has its interest tied to a stock market-related index.

37. Joanna and her husband, Bill, have a $40,000 annuity that pays them $200 a month. Bill dies and Joanna continues receiving the $200 monthly check as long as she lives. When Joanna dies, the company ceases payment. This is an example of a(n)

    A. installment refund annuity
    B. joint and full survivor annuity
    C. life annuity
    D. cash refund annuity

Answers & Rationale

1.   **D.**   Unlike life insurance, an annuity is used primarily to provide income during life; consequently, annuity payments are guaranteed to be paid as long as the annuitant lives.
QID: 1297

2.   **C.**   The principal function of life insurance is to create an estate. The principal function of annuities is to liquidate an estate.
QID: 1298

3.   **D.**   Annuities are classified by method of payment, number of lives covered, disposition of proceeds and various other methods.
QID: 1299

4.   **B.**   Typically, annuity payments are made on a monthly basis to the annuitant.
QID: 1300

5.   **D.**   Age, sex, expenses (plus premium contributions, payment cost, interest rate and type of annuity option selected) are factors that determine the annuity benefit. The annuitant's tax bracket is not a factor.
QID: 1301

6.   **B.**   The accumulation period is that time during which funds are being paid into the annuity, in the form of premiums by the contract holder and interest earnings credited by the insurer. The payout or annuity period refers to the point at which the annuity ceases to be an accumulation vehicle and begins to generate income payments on a regular basis.
QID: 1302

7.   **A.**   Age, sex and assumed interest rate are annuity premium factors; medical history is not. Annuities do not require any medical underwriting for issuance.
QID: 1303

8.   **A.**   If both an older and younger person had annuity funds of the same amount and simultaneously began to receive monthly payments, the older person would receive the larger payments since the insurer would expect to pay the older person for a shorter time according to life expectancy.
QID: 1304

9.   **B.**   If other factors are equal, a higher assumed interest rate credited to the accumulation units results in a lower investment from the variable annuity owner.
QID: 1305

10.   **D.**   The loading factor in annuities takes into consideration the agents' commissions, clerical support and other general costs of doing business.
QID: 1306

11.   **B.**   A refund annuity guarantees a specific amount of benefits, which will be paid regardless of whether the annuitant is alive to receive them. If the annuitant dies before receiving this minimum guaranteed benefit, the money is paid to a beneficiary or to the estate.
QID: 1307

12.   **A.**   The annuitant can be compared to an insured in a life insurance policy. The annuitant is the person by whose life the contract is measured. Just as life insurance policyowners are often the insureds, annuity owners are often the annuitants.
QID: 1308

13.   **D.**   Annuities are designed to liquidate a principal sum over the lifetime of the annuitant. In essence, they protect against an individual outliving his or her income. They are not designed to protect against the uncertainty of death, as is life insurance. They are not intended to provide temporary relief due to unemployment.
QID: 1309

14.   **B.**   Since an immediate annuity makes its first payment at the first payment from the date of purchase, and since most annuities make monthly payments, an immediate annuity would typically

pay its first payment one month from the purchase date. Thus, an immediate annuity has a relatively short accumulation period.
QID: 1310

15. D. Unlike a fixed annuity, a variable annuity guarantees neither the rate of return the annuity fund will earn, nor the amount of benefit payments the annuitant will receive. Both are dependent on how well the variable annuity's underlying investments perform.
QID: 1311

16. D. A period certain option guarantees payments for a certain amount of time, whether or not the annuitant is alive. The payments stop when the specified period is over. A straight life option pays the annuitant a guaranteed income for his or her lifetime. No further payments are made after the annuitant dies. An installment refund option pays out what is left to the beneficiary in the form of continued annuity payments.
QID: 1312

17. D. Annuities may be purchased with a single lump-sum, a scheduled payment or a flexible payment.
QID: 1313

18. D. If an annuitant has a cash refund annuity and dies after the annuity income begins, his or her beneficiary will receive a lump-sum cash payment equal to the annuity fund, less the amount of income already paid the deceased.
QID: 1314

19. A. A single premium annuity is funded with one payment. When the funding is provided with a single, lump sum, the principal is created immediately.
QID: 1315

20. A. Annuities can be classified as immediate or deferred, depending on when benefits begin. An immediate annuity begins benefit payouts one payment interval following the annuitant's initial payment to the company. Immediate annuities are

always purchased with a single payment. In contrast, a deferred annuity begins benefit payouts after a period longer than one payment interval.
QID: 1316

21. B. Also known as the "life income with term certain" option, this payout approach is designed to pay the annuitant an income for life, but guarantees a definite period of payments. If an individual has a ten-year life with period certain annuity, and receives monthly payments for six years before dying, his or her beneficiary will receive the same payments for four more years.
QID: 1317

22. A. When an individual owning a pure life annuity dies, no further payments are made. Of the settlement arrangements listed, a pure life annuity generates the largest monthly income.
QID: 1318

23. B. Under the installment refund annuity, the beneficiary receives the same monthly income (minus payments previously paid to the original annuitant) until the face amount is exhausted. In this case, the original $25,000 annuity fund has paid $12,960, leaving $12,040 for Lucy.
QID: 1319

24. C. An installment refund annuity assumes that the total annuity fund will be paid to the annuitant, his or her beneficiary, or both.
QID: 1320

25. A. Of these options, only the cash refund payout guarantees that the entire annuity principal will be paid out to the annuitant or beneficiary. A pure life option and a period certain option guarantee payments for a certain period of time, during which principal may or may not be fully liquidated.
QID: 1321

26. A. The survivor under a joint and full survivor annuity receives 100 percent of the original joint income. Under an installment refund annuity, when the original annuitant dies, the same income will be paid to the beneficiary until the full annuity face amount has been paid. A straight life

income annuity pays out only during the lifetime of the annuitant and has no provisions for payments to a beneficiary.
QID: 1322

27. C.   If the net contribution to a variable annuity account is $350 and the cost of one accumulation unit is $87.50, four units would be assigned to the account ($350 divided by $87.50 equals 4).
QID: 1323

28. C.   During the accumulation period of a deferred variable annuity, the value of the individual account rises or falls based on the investment results of the annuity's underlying securities.
QID: 1324

29. C.   A variable annuity with 2,500 accumulation units, each valued at $3, is worth $7,500 (2,500 x $3 = $7,500).
QID: 1325

30. B.   Each annuity payment consists of both principal and interest. The principal amount is comprised of after-tax dollars, and is not taxed when paid. The interest amount is taxable as ordinary income.
QID: 1326

31. A.   Employees of nonprofit charitable, educational and religious organizations may participate in tax-sheltered annuity (TSA) plans.
QID: 1327

32. B.   Tax-sheltered annuities are available to employees of certain nonprofit organizations, such as schools. Participants do not pay current taxes on their contributions, but will be taxed on benefits when they are received.
QID: 1328

33. A.   An exclusion ratio is applied to each benefit payment the annuitant receives to determine the amount that is excluded from taxation investment in the contract is equal to exclusion

ratio divided by expected return. The investment in the contract is the amount of money paid into the annuity. The expected return is the annual guaranteed benefit the annuitant receives, multiplied by the number of years he or she will receive benefits.
QID: 1329

34. B.   Section 1035 of the Internal Revenue Code provides for tax-free exchanges of certain kinds of financial products, including the exchange of life insurance for annuity contracts.
QID: 1330

35. A.   The income flow from immediate annuities can be either fixed or variable. With a fixed immediate annuity, the annuitant is guaranteed an income flow without risk of market fluctuations affecting the amount of income. With a variable immediate annuity, the investment risk is transferred to the annuitant. This means that once an income stream is created, the payments can increase or decrease depending on the performance of the underlying investments.
QID: 3328

36. D.   An equity indexed annuity has most of the features of fixed annuity contracts except that the interest credited to the annuity owner's account is tied to a stock market-related index, such as the Standard & Poor's 500 Index. Unlike variable annuities, an equity indexed annuity cannot decrease in value and has a fixed minimum guarantee.
QID: 3329

37. B.   The joint and full survivor option provides for payment of the annuity to two people. If either person dies, the same income payments continue to the survivor for life. When the surviving annuitant dies, no further payments are made to anyone.
QID: 3330

Retirement Plans

1. For tax purposes, retirement plans can be divided into which of the following two categories?

   A. Fixed and variable
   B. Whole and term
   C. Qualified and nonqualified
   D. Independent and funded

2. What entity qualifies retirement plans?

   A. Insurance company underwriting the fund
   B. State insurance department
   C. Federal government
   D. Sponsoring employer

3. All of the following statements concerning qualified retirement plans are correct EXCEPT

   A. employer contributions to a qualified plan are tax deductible as a business expense
   B. employer contributions to a qualified plan on behalf of its employees are taxable income to the employees when they are made
   C. the earnings of a qualified plan are not taxed until they are distributed
   D. employer-sponsored IRAs are considered qualified retirement plans

4. Many of the basic concepts associated with qualified employer plans can be traced to the

   A. Social Security Reform Act
   B. McCarren-Ferguson Act
   C. Employee Retirement Income Security Act
   D. Public Law 15

5. Wendell, age 57, last year withdrew $1,500 from his traditional IRA, which consists entirely of pre-tax contributions. In addition to including that amount in his taxable income, he has to pay a penalty of

   A. $50
   B. $100
   C. $150
   D. $300

6. The penalty for premature withdrawal of funds from a traditional IRA is

   A. 5 percent or $50, whichever is less
   B. 10 percent of the account balance
   C. 10 percent of the taxable amount withdrawn
   D. $100

7. David is age 40 and single. He earned $45,000 in the year 2001 as an engineer with a company that has a group health plan but no employer-sponsored retirement plan. David set up a Traditional IRA in 2001. What is the maximum contribution he can deduct from taxes that year?

    A. $1,000
    B. $2,000
    C. $2,250
    D. $4,000

8. Oliver is age 35, married and earns an adjusted gross income of $155,000 annually as an aerospace engineer. His wife is also employed and files jointly. Both are covered by their companies' pension plans. Therefore, Oliver is entitled to deduct contributions to a traditional IRA of up to

    A. $0
    B. $250
    C. $2,250
    D. $4,000

9. All of the following employed persons who have no employer retirement plan would be eligible to set up a traditional IRA EXCEPT

    A. Miriam, age 26, a secretary
    B. Brent, age 40, a medical technician
    C. Edna, age 72, a nurse
    D. Jack, age 60, a plumber

10. Lee, age 66, is not covered by an employer retirement plan. In 2001, he will have a gross income of $22,000 from investments, $1,500 from working part-time for a former employer and $7,200 from Social Security. The maximum deductible contribution he can make to a traditional IRA in 2001 is

    A. $1,500
    B. $2,000
    C. $2,200
    D. $3,000

11. Max, age 32, is employed as an architect and earns a salary of $55,000 in 2001. He is covered by his company's corporate retirement plan. What is the maximum amount he can contribute to an IRA that year?

    A. $0
    B. $1,500
    C. $2,000
    D. $5,500

12. Herbert and Olga have been married 10 years. They have no children and each has a well-paying job. However, neither is covered by an employer retirement plan. What is the maximum amount they could set aside in tax-deductible IRA funds during 2001 for retirement?

    A. $2,000
    B. $2,250
    C. $3,000
    D. $4,000

13. All of the following statements pertaining to spousal IRAs are correct EXCEPT

    A. an eligible working spouse may set up such a plan with a nonworking spouse
    B. the maximum annual combined deductible contribution permitted is $2,250 for 2001
    C. the annual contribution must be split into two accounts, with a maximum of $2,000 contributed into one account for any year the plan exists
    D. a spousal IRA contribution must be reported on a joint tax return

14. Rodney, who earned $40,000 in 2000 and did not participate in an employer retirement plan, has a nonworking spouse. They filed a joint income tax return. Which of the following statements applies?

    A. Rodney could establish a separate IRA for himself and another for his wife, and deduct a contribution of up to $4,000 for 2000.
    B. Rodney could establish an IRA for himself, but not for his wife because she is unemployed. However, because he is married, he could contribute and deduct up to twice the maximum for an individual IRA, or $4,000.
    C. Rodney could establish an IRA for himself and contribute any amount he wishes to it.
    D. Rodney could establish separate IRAs for himself and his wife and contribute and deduct $4,000 to his and $2,000 to his wife's.

15. Acme, Inc. has established a qualified plan that provides retiring employees with a benefit equal to one percent for each of the employee's years of service, times his or her final pay, as averaged over the last five years of employment. What kind of plan has Acme installed?

    A. Defined contribution
    B. Profit sharing
    C. Stock bonus
    D. Defined benefit

16. Cynthia is scheduled to receive a $36,000 lump-sum distribution from her former employer's qualified pension plan and wishes to establish a rollover IRA to avoid paying taxes on the money that year. Within how many days must the rollover be completed to avoid paying taxes?

    A. 30 days
    B. 60 days
    C. 90 days
    D. 120 days

17. All of the following statements pertaining to traditional IRAs are correct EXCEPT

    A. June has accumulated $30,000 of pre-tax dollars and earnings in her traditional IRA. At age 55 she withdraws $2,500 to take a vacation. She will have to include the $2,500 in her taxable income for the year and pay a $250 penalty.
    B. Bradley has $36,000 of pre-tax dollars and earnings in a traditional IRA when he decides to retire, and he elects to withdraw $8,000 per year. In his first year of retirement, $8,000 will be included in his taxable income.
    C. Peter inherits $15,000 in traditional IRA benefits from his father, who died in 1999. Peter can set up a tax-favored rollover traditional IRA with the money.
    D. Walter is age 60 and not disabled. If he takes a distribution from his traditional IRA, it is subject to tax as ordinary income, but with no penalty for early withdrawal.

18. A primary difference between a SEP and an IRA is that

    A. the amount an employer can contributed to a SEP is unlimited
    B. the employer can contribute to an IRA but not to a SEP
    C. the limit of money an employer is permitted to contribute to a SEP each year is higher than what can be contributed to an IRA
    D. the amount contributed by an employer to a SEP is included in the employee's gross income

19. An employer's maximum annual contribution for an employee to a simplified employee pension (SEP) in 2001 is

    A. the lesser of 15 percent of compensation or $35,000
    B. a flat $35,000
    C. the lesser of 25 percent of compensation or $35,000
    D. 25 percent of compensation or $25,000, whichever is less

20. All of the following statements pertaining to SIMPLE plans are correct EXCEPT

    A. SIMPLE plans allow employers to set up tax-favored retirement savings plans for their employees without having to comply with complicated qualification requirements
    B. these plans are reserved for employers with 500 or more employees
    C. SIMPLE plans may be structured like IRAs or 401(k) plans
    D. all employees are fully and immediately vested in SIMPLE plans

21. If an owner-employee's adjusted gross income during 2001 is $48,000, what is the maximum amount he or she could contribute to a defined contribution retirement plan?

    A. $4,800
    B. $12,000
    C. $14,400
    D. $24,000

22. All of the following should be eligible to establish a Keogh retirement plan EXCEPT

    A. a dentist in private practice
    B. partners in a furniture store
    C. the sole proprietor of a jewelry store
    D. a major stockholder-employee in a family corporation

23. Oliver, a surgeon, has an adjusted gross income of $175,000. The maximum contribution he may make to his defined contribution plan for the year 2001 is

    A. $0
    B. $26,250
    C. $35,000
    D. $43,750

24. Which of the following types of plans would fall under the minimum funding rules of the Internal Revenue Code?

    A. Pension
    B. Profit sharing
    C. 401(k)
    D. Stock bonus

25. The combination of current tax deduction for the employer plus tax deferral for the employee is possible with all of the following types of plans EXCEPT

    A. Stock bonus
    B. Money purchase
    C. Savings account
    D. 401(k)

26. Section 457 of the Internal Revenue Code establishes rules for deferred compensation plans for

    A. collectively bargained agreements
    B. state and local governments
    C. multi-employer trusts
    D. employee-owned public corporations

27. Which of the following statements pertaining to qualified corporate retirement plans is NOT correct?

    A. The two types of qualified corporate retirement plans are defined benefit and defined contribution.
    B. Contributions to a qualified corporate retirement plan made by the employer are deductible as a business expense.
    C. Ron participates in his company's qualified retirement plan, which will provide a benefit of two percent of his salary for each year he participates in the plan. This is an example of a defined contribution plan.
    D. A defined contribution plan does not have to provide a definitely determinable future benefit to maintain qualified status.

28. The advantages of qualified retirement plans to employers include all of the following EXCEPT

    A. favorable tax rules
    B. increased employee productivity
    C. reward a few employees rather than many
    D. allows the employer to attract and keep talented employees

29. Which of the following plans provides for specified amounts going into the plan currently and identifies the participant's interest and vested balance?

    A. Defined contribution
    B. Defined benefit
    C. Cash arrangement
    D. Deferred arrangement

30. Which of the following plans allows employees to elect to take a reduction in their current salaries by deferring amounts into a retirement plan?

    A. IRA
    B. Keogh
    C. Defined contribution
    D. 401(k)

31. Which of the following statements pertaining to Social Security benefits is CORRECT?

    A. Only individuals who have paid into the Social Security system are eligible to receive Social Security benefits.
    B. Social Security taxes are payable on all of an individual's income from whatever source.
    C. Social Security pays benefits in the event of retirement or death only.
    D. Both employees and employers are taxed to pay for Social Security.

32. To be eligible for death, retirement or disability benefits under Social Security, a worker must be

    A. completely insured
    B. currently insured
    C. fully insured
    D. partially insured

33. Which of the following statements is CORRECT?

    A. Lester, age 25, who recently became totally and permanently disabled, may qualify for Social Security benefits, as long as he is classified as currently insured.
    B. Continuing to work after retirement will have no effect on a retiree's Social Security benefits.
    C. When an eligible worker dies, Social Security does not provide death benefits to surviving dependents when an eligible worker survives.
    D. The Social Security program is funded by a payroll tax.

34. At age 65, a fully insured retired worker is entitled to full Social Security benefits. This equals 100 percent of which of the following?

    A. PIA
    B. AMW
    C. MFB
    D. AIME

35. All of the following are allowable reasons to take an early withdrawal from an IRA and NOT pay a tax penalty EXCEPT

    A. purchase of a vacation home
    B. death
    C. disability
    D. qualifying medical expense

36. Which of the following statements about a Roth IRA is CORRECT?

    A. The maximum annual contribution for 2001 is $2,000, regardless of contributions to a traditional IRA.
    B. Contributions are not deductible.
    C. Only individuals younger than age 70 ½ can contribute.
    D. Distributions must begin at age 70 ½.

37. Which of the following distributions from a Roth IRA would be qualified and, therefore, NOT taxable assuming the account was established at least five years ago?

    A. A distribution made before age 59 ½, provided the recipient is retired
    B. A distribution used to pay costs of a college education
    C. A distribution used to purchase a vacation home
    D. A distribution made before age 55 ½.

38. Which of the following expenses may be covered by an education IRA?

    A. Costs of a college education
    B. Costs of ground and flight school
    C. Costs of a weekend computer seminar
    D. Costs of a private high school

39. Arthur and Donna establish an education IRA for their son, Anthony. Although Anthony attends college full time and graduates, the IRA still contains some funds. Which of the following would be the only way for Arthur, Donna and Anthony to dispose of these remaining funds without incurring a tax penalty?

    A. Distribute the funds to Anthony
    B. Roll over the funds to another education IRA established for Anthony's younger sister Mary, who is 20.
    C. Substitute their daughter, Mary, as the beneficiary and use the funds to pay for her high school education
    D. Withdraw the funds and close the account

40. All of the following statements about Social Security retirement benefits are correct EXCEPT

    A. Earnings are permanently reduced for individuals who retire early and receive benefits.
    B. Greater benefits are available for individuals who delay retirement beyond their normal retirement age.
    C. The normal retirement age for receiving Social Security benefits will gradually increase from age 65.
    D. Fully insured workers are eligible for full retirement income benefits beginning at age 62.

41. Brad, age 67, works part-time and earned $20,000 this year. He also began receiving Social Security benefits this year. Which of the following statements is CORRECT?

   A. Brad's Social Security benefits will be permanently reduced because he fails the earnings test.
   B. Brad can receive full Social Security benefits, with no limit on his earnings.
   C. For every $2 earned above the annual limit, $1 will be deducted from Brad's earnings.
   D. Brad can receive full Social Security benefits, provided that his earnings do not exceed the annual limit.

42. All of the following benefits are available under Social Security EXCEPT

   A. welfare benefits
   B. death benefits
   C. old-age or retirement benefits
   D. disability benefits

43. All of the following statements about SIMPLE plans are correct EXCEPT

   A. They may be structured as an IRA or a 401(k) cash or deferred arrangement.
   B. Only employers with 100 or fewer employees can establish SIMPLE plans.
   C. The employer can offer both a SIMPLE plan and another qualified plan.
   D. The employer must make either a dollar-for-dollar matching contribution or a nonelective contribution of 2 percent of compensation.

44. Which of the following statements about contributions to a qualified plan is CORRECT?

   A. Employer contributions are 100 percent vested when made.
   B. Employees have nonforfeitable rights in both employee and employer contributions when made.
   C. Employees have a 100 percent vested interest in benefits made from their own contributions.
   D. Employers have the option of creating vesting schedules for benefits.

45. All of the following statements about Section 457 deferred compensation plans are correct EXCEPT

   A. They can be created for employees of state and local governments and non-profit organizations.
   B. Amounts deferred under these plans are not subject to current taxation.
   C. Life insurance and annuities are authorized investments for these plans.
   D. The maximum amount that an employee can defer is $10,500.

46. Bill is self-employed and earned $10,000 in 2001. How much can he contribute to his SIMPLE IRA this year?

   A. $2,000
   B. $5,000
   C. $6,500
   D. $10,000

47. Susan, age 52, withdrew $5,000 from her traditional IRA which consisted entirely of pre-tax contributions to purchase her first condo. What are the tax consequences?

    A. Susan must pay a 10 percent penalty tax on the withdrawal.
    B. Susan must pay a 10 percent penalty tax plus income tax on the withdrawal.
    C. Susan will not be assessed a 10 percent penalty tax if she pays back the withdrawal within 60 days.
    D. Susan will not be assessed the 10 percent penalty tax on her early withdrawal.

48. What are the tax consequences if Bob makes a partial rollover of his 401(k) plan assets?

    A. Bob must only pay a 10 percent penalty tax on the amount retained.
    B. Bob must pay a 10 percent penalty tax plus income tax on the amount retained.
    C. Bob must only pay income tax on the amount retained.
    D. Because partial rollovers are permitted, Bob does not have to pay income tax or the 10 percent penalty tax on the amount retained

Answers & Rationale

1.   C.   For tax purposes, retirement plans can be divided into two categories qualified, which meet certain IRS standards, and nonqualified, which do not require IRS approval.
QID: 1331

2.   C.   Qualified plans are those that meet requirements established by the federal government and, consequently, receive favorable tax treatment.
QID: 1332

3.   B.   Employer contributions to a qualified plan on behalf of its employees are not considered taxable income to the employees when they are made.
QID: 1333

4.   C.   The Employee Retirement Income Security Act of 1974, commonly known as ERISA, protects the rights of workers covered under an employer-sponsored plan. ERISA imposes a number of requirements that retirement plans must follow to obtain IRS approval as qualified plans.
QID: 1334

5.   C.   When prematurely withdrawing pre-tax dollars from an IRA (before reaching age 59 ½), the individual must include the amount withdrawn in his or her taxable income as well as pay a penalty equal to 10 percent of the taxable amount withdrawn. There are exceptions which allow an individual to withdraw funds before age 59 ½ without paying a penalty for a life annuity, to buy a first home, for education costs, disability, or upon the owner's death. After age 59 ½, any IRA distribution is taxed as ordinary income with no penalty.
QID: 1335

6.   C.   A premature withdrawal is generally taken before the owner reaches age 59 ½ and carries adverse tax consequences. The penalty for premature withdrawal of funds from a traditional IRA is 10 percent of the taxable amount withdrawn.
QID: 1336

7.   B.   Because the individual in this problem has no company retirement plan, he is eligible to set up an IRA and deduct $2,000, the maximum amount. The contribution limit is scheduled to increase to $3,000 for 2002–2004, $4,000 for 2005–2007 and $5,000 for 2008 and beyond.
QID: 1337

8.   A.   A married person loses IRA deductibility when the couple's joint income exceeds the maximum-indexed amount of $62,000, both spouses file jointly, and both are covered under a qualified retirement plan.
QID: 1338

9.   C.   Individuals must be under age 70 ½ to be eligible for a traditional IRA.
QID: 1339

10.   A.   Only income received as compensation for services is eligible for a traditional IRA contribution. Compensation includes wages, salaries, fees, commissions, tips and bonuses. It does not include retirement income or earned interest. In this case, although Lee earned $30,700 for the year, only $1,500 is compensation. Because Lee is not covered by an employer plan and he is under age 70 ½, he can contribute and deduct the full $1,500, which at 100 percent of his earned income is still less than the maximum limit in 2001 of $2,000 or 100 percent of compensation, whichever is less.
QID: 1340

11.   C.   Anyone who is under age 70 ½ and who has earned income may contribute to an IRA, up to an annual maximum in 2001 of $2,000 or 100 percent of income, whichever is less. It is the deductibility of the contribution that is affected by the taxpayer's earnings and by his or her participation in a corporate retirement plan.
QID: 1341

12. D. Married couples who work and are without employer pension coverage may establish IRAs and deduct annual contributions up to a total of $4,000 in 2001. The annual contribution limit for such married couples is scheduled to increase to $6,000 for 2002–2004, $8,000 for 2005–2007 and $10,000 for 2008 and beyond.
QID: 1342

13. B. Spousal IRAs can be established for married couples when one works and the other does not (or the other earns less than $250). A maximum deductible contribution of $4,000 (the 2001 limit) can be made when the working spouse is not covered by an employer's retirement plan. The contribution must be split between two accounts and the couple must file a joint income tax return that shows their respective contributions.
QID: 1343

14. A. The spousal deduction is available for qualified taxpayers for separate IRA accounts one belonging to the taxpayer, the other, to the spouse. The maximum deductible amount in 2000 was $4,000, with a maximum of $2,000 contributed to each account.
QID: 1344

15. D. A defined benefit plan specifies the amount of benefit promised to the retiree at retirement. It does not specify the amount the employer must contribute; instead, the amount of contribution that must be made to fund the future benefit is calculated annually to assure that the plan will have sufficient funds to pay benefits as each participant retires.
QID: 1345

16. B. A maximum of 60 days is allowed to complete a rollover to an IRA before the IRS will tax an individual on a lump-sum distribution.
QID: 1346

17. C. Only the individual who establishes the traditional IRA and his or her spouse are eligible to benefit from the rollover treatment.
QID: 1347

18. C. A SEP is an arrangement whereby an employee establishes and maintains an individual retirement account, to which the employer contributes. Employer contributions are not included in the employee's gross income. A primary difference between a SEP and an IRA is the much larger amount that can be contributed each year to a SEP—up to 15 percent of the employee's compensation or $35,000 (as of Jan. 1 2001), whichever is less. This limit is much higher than that of an IRA.
QID: 1348

19. A. An employer's maximum annual contribution for an employee to a simplified employee pension (SEP) is the lesser of 15 percent of compensation or $35,000 (as of Jan. 1, 2001). Note that the compensation or earned income in excess of $170,000 is not taken into account. Therefore, the 15 percent of compensation limit is effectively placed at $25,500 (or $170,000 x 15%). The plan must include every eligible employee.
QID: 1349

20. B. SIMPLE plans are reserved to small business that employ 100 or fewer employees.
QID: 1350

21. B. The current maximum allowable annual contribution to a defined contribution retirement plan is the lesser of 25 percent of after-contribution earnings or $35,000 (as of Jan. 1, 2001). Thus, if an owner-employee's adjusted gross income is $48,000, the maximum amount he or she could contribute to a defined contribution retirement plan is $12,000. In 2002, the maximum annual contribution is scheduled to increase to $40,000.
QID: 1351

22. D. Keogh are designed for self-employed individuals, not a stockholder-employee in a family corporation.
QID: 1352

23. C. The current maximum allowable annual contribution to a Keogh retirement plan is the lesser of 25 percent of after-contribution earnings or $35,000 (as of January 1, 2001). Thus, if Oliver's

adjusted gross income is $175,000, the maximum amount he can contribute to a Keogh plan is $35,000.
QID: 1353

24. A. Since a pension plan is designed to provide a definitely determinable future benefit, the employer must keep the plan's funds at an adequate level at all times, subject to minimum funding standards. Since profit-sharing, 401(k) and stock bonus plans promise no specific future benefit, they are not subject to the minimum funding standards (though there must be substantial and recurring contributions to the plan or it will be deemed terminated).
QID: 1354

25. C. The combination of current tax deductibility by the employer and tax deferral for the employee is the primary tax benefit of all qualified plans, of which stock bonus and money purchase are two types.
QID: 1355

26. B. Section 457 covers rules for the taxation of participants in deferred compensation plans of state and local governments and non-profit organizations. If a plan is eligible under Section 457, deferred compensation will not be included in gross income until it is actually received or made available. Life insurance and annuities are authorized investments for these plans.
QID: 1356

27. C. The third answer choice describes a defined benefit plan, which is designed to provide a definitely determinable benefit at some future date.
QID: 1357

28. C. Qualified retirement plans provide many advantages to employers including favorable tax rules, increased productivity from employees and good public relations with employees and the public.
QID: 1358

29. A. The provisions of a defined contribution plan cover amounts going into the plan currently and identify the participant's interest and vested balance.
QID: 1359

30. D. The 401(k) plans allow employees to reduce their current salaries by deferring amounts into a retirement plan. These plans are called "cash or deferred arrangements" because employees cannot be forced to participate; they may take their income currently as cash, or defer a portion of it until retirement, with favorable tax advantages. The deferred amounts are not included in the employees' gross income and earnings credited to the deferrals grow tax free until distribution.
QID: 1360

31. D. Social Security was designed to provide benefits to individuals and their families in the event of death, disability or retirement. It can cover all members of an eligible worker's family, whether or not they themselves have paid into the system. Social Security is funded by a tax on a worker's pay, which is shared equally by the worker and the employer.
QID: 1361

32. C. To be eligible for death, retirement or disability benefits under Social Security, a worker must be "fully insured." To qualify as fully insured, an individual must have one quarter of coverage for each calendar year that has elapsed after 1950 up to the year he or she becomes eligible for benefits, with no fewer than six quarters.
QID: 1362

33. D. To be eligible for disability benefits under Social Security, an individual needs to be qualified as "fully insured," not "currently insured." In addition, working has a significant effect on a retiree's Social Security benefits. Retirees who continue to work and earn wages after their Social Security benefits begin are limited as to the amount of wages they can receive. If they

exceed this "earnings limit," their benefits are reduced. Social Security does provide death benefits to surviving dependents.
QID: 1363

34.   A.   The PIA (Primary Insurance Amount) is equal to the worker's full retirement benefit. Social Security will pay this amount at full retirement age to a fully insured, retired worker.
QID: 1364

35.   A.   If an IRA owner who is younger than 59 ½ withdraws money from an IRA, he or she must pay a tax penalty of 10 percent of the amount withdrawn, except in cases of death, disability or for qualifying medical expenses. Taking the money out of an IRA to buy a vacation home would require the IRA owner to pay the penalty tax.
QID: 1365

36.   B.   Although contributions to a Roth IRA are not deductible, interest, dividends and capital gains accumulate tax free. An individual may set up a Roth IRA and contribute to a traditional IRA, but annual contributions to all IRAs cannot exceed $2,000 in 2001. Unlike traditional IRAs, there is no prohibition on making contributions after reaching age 70 ½ and distributions need not begin at age 70 ½.
QID: 1366

37.   B.   A qualified distribution (one that is not taxed) is made after the taxpayer reaches age 59 ½, made to a beneficiary after the taxpayer's death, made because the taxpayer is disabled, used to buy the taxpayer's first home, or used to pay education costs. Furthermore, the distribution cannot be made any earlier than five years after the account was set up.
QID: 1367

38.   A.   Education IRAs are special investment accounts for funding a college education, including tuition, fees, books, supplies and equipment, and room and board, provided the student

attends school at least half time. Qualified expenses also include those related to graduate level courses.
QID: 1368

39.   B.   Education IRAs are special accounts to fund college and post-graduate study. If a child for whom an account is established does not attend college or if there are funds remaining in an account when the beneficiary turns 30, these funds may be rolled over to another education IRA that benefits another family member (account owner, spouse, child or grandchild) with no penalty. The new recipient must be under the age of 30. Any IRA distributions that are not used to pay for a beneficiary's college or post-graduate education expenses will be included in the recipient's income and will be subject to a 10 percent penalty. Therefore, in this scenario, the second answer choice describes the only way to dispose of the funds without incurring a tax penalty.
QID: 1369

40.   D.   Fully insured workers are eligible for full retirement income benefits at their full retirement age. Permanently reduced benefits are available from age 62 for those who elect to retire early and draw benefits; slightly greater benefits are available for those who delay retirement beyond age 65. Because of longer life expectancies, the normal retirement age will gradually increase.
QID: 3331

41.   B.   Under prior law, anyone under age 70 who was receiving Social Security retirement benefits but continued to work could earn only so much each year without having benefits reduced. Beginning in 2001, this law was repealed. Under the new rules, starting with the month a person reaches full retirement age, he or she can continue working and receive Social Security benefits, with no limit on earnings. If a person is under the full retirement age when he or she begins receiving Social Security benefits and continues to work, his or her benefits will still be reduced.
QID: 3332

42. A. Social Security provides death benefits, old-age or retirement benefits and disability benefits to eligible workers. Social Security is an entitlement program, not a welfare program.
QID: 3333

43. C. Employers with 100 or fewer employees can establish SIMPLE plans. However, the employer cannot have another qualified plan in place. SIMPLE plans can be structured as an IRA or a 401(k) cash or deferred arrangement. Employees can defer up to a specified amount each year and the employer then makes a matching contribution, dollar-for-dollar, up to an amount equal to 3 percent of the employee's annual compensation. Alternatively, the employer may make nonelective contributions of 2 percent of the employee's compensation.
QID: 3334

44. C. All qualified plans must meet standards that set forth the employee vesting schedule and nonforfeitable rights at any specified time. For all plans, an employee always has a 100 percent vested interest in benefits that accrue from his or her own contributions. Benefits that accrue from employer contributions must vest according to vesting schedules established by law.
QID: 3335

45. D. State and local governments and non-profit organizations can establish Section 457 deferred compensation plans for their employees. Amounts deferred are not included in gross income until they are actually received or made available. Life insurance and annuities are authorized investments for these plans. Employees may defer the lesser of $8,500 in 2001 or 33 1/3 percent of includable compensation.
QID: 3336

46. C. In 2001, employees can contribute up to $6,500 to their SIMPLE plan accounts. Bill's contribution is therefore limited to $6,500.
QID: 3337

47. D. With few exceptions, any distribution from a traditional IRA before age 59 ½ will be subject to income tax and a 10 percent penalty tax. However, up to $10,000 may be withdrawn before age 59 ½ to pay for first-time home expenses without being assessed the 10 percent penalty.
QID: 3338

48. B. Distributions from employer-sponsored plans are eligible for a tax-free rollover if reinvested in an IRA within 60 days after receipt of the distribution and if the plan participant does not actually take physical receipt of the distribution. The entire amount need not be rolled over; a partial distribution may be rolled over from one IRA or eligible plan to another IRA. However, if a partial rollover is executed, the part retained will be taxed as ordinary income and subject to a 10 percent tax.
QID: 3339

10

Life Underwriting and Policy Delivery

1. What is the most common approach for "rating" life insurance applicants who are determined to be substandard risks?

   A. Issuing a policy in the amount applied for, with a higher than standard premium
   B. Issuing a policy of less than applied for, with a lower than standard premium
   C. Issuing a policy in the amount applied for, but reducing the amount paid out as a death benefit
   D. Issuing a policy in the amount applied for, but crediting its values with lower interest rates

2. Underwriting is a process of

   A. selecting and marketing policies
   B. determining and establishing premiums
   C. selecting, reporting and rejecting risks
   D. selecting, classifying and rating risks

3. Which of the following terms describes policies issued to men and women based on the same premium ratings?

   A. Neutral
   B. Sexist
   C. Unisex
   D. Multi-line

4. With regard to life insurance applications, which of the following statements is CORRECT?

   A. All applications for life insurance must include a medical exam.
   B. The application includes the names of the insured and beneficiary.
   C. Part I of the application deals with the proposed insured's medical history.
   D. Part II of the application deals with the proposed insured's personal and occupational history.

5. All of the following are sources of insurability information about life insurance applicants EXCEPT

   A. Social Security reports
   B. inspection reports
   C. Medical Information Bureau
   D. the application

6. Which section of the application SHOULD contain a record of any injuries the applicant may have suffered?

   A. Medical section
   B. Agent's report
   C. Special questionnaire
   D. MIB

7. If a medical report is required on an applicant, it is completed by

   A. a home office underwriter
   B. a paramedic or examining physician
   C. the agent
   D. the home office medical director

8. When applicable, all of the following forms require an applicant's signature EXCEPT

   A. aviation questionnaire
   B. authorization form
   C. agent's report
   D. application

9. Which of the following statements pertaining to sources of insurability information is CORRECT?

   A. The insurance agent completes the medical report on a life insurance applicant.
   B. Special questionnaires are used to obtain additional information when an extra hazard or risk may be involved, and to replace the application in unusual cases.
   C. An insurer cannot use an unfavorable credit report to reject an applicant for insurance.
   D. When conducting an inspection report, an investigator cannot interview an individual who actually knows the applicant.

10. Angela, a recent applicant for a $50,000 life insurance policy, failed to state on her application that she suffered a heart attack a year earlier, fearing it would affect her insurability. Angela violated which of the following?

    A. Doctrine of warranties
    B. Doctrine of interpretation
    C. Doctrine of indemnity
    D. Doctrine of concealment

11. All of the following statements pertaining to life insurance are correct EXCEPT

    A. The underwriter wants to check with a doctor concerning an applicant's past hospital treatment, but does not receive a signed authorization. The agent likely will be asked to obtain the signed authorization.
    B. Kyle wonders if his policy is voided when the company learns his parents died in a train wreck rather than a plane, as he stated on his application. The policy can be canceled because statements on the application are warranties and not representations.
    C. The ABC Co. applies for a life insurance policy on the life of its general sales manager. From the standpoint of insurable risk, the application likely will be approved.
    D. Margaret applies for a policy on the life of a friend. From the standpoint of insurable interest, the application probably will be rejected.

12. All of the following statements pertaining to the Medical Information Bureau (MIB) are correct EXCEPT

    A. The purpose of the MIB is to help prevent fraud and to serve as a reliable source of important medical information about insurance applicants.
    B. The MIB is organized and supported by private hospitals.
    C. Applicants for life insurance must be informed in writing that the insurer may make a report on their health to the MIB.
    D. Applicants must sign authorization forms for information from the MIB files to be given to a member company.

13. Which of the following statements pertaining to the Medical Information Bureau (MIB) is CORRECT?

    A. Information obtained in connection with life insurance claims is reported to the MIB.
    B. Information obtained by the MIB is available to all physicians.
    C. Information obtained by the MIB is sold to any interested parties.
    D. Information obtained by the MIB may be used by an insurer to decide whether to insure an applicant.

14. All of the following statements pertaining to inspection reports on life insurance applicants are correct EXCEPT

    A. They help to determine the insurability of applicants.
    B. They provide information obtained principally from law enforcement officials.
    C. They generally are requested on applicants who apply for large amounts of life insurance.
    D. They usually are obtained from national investigative agencies or firms.

15. All of the following statements pertaining to inspection reports and credit reports on life insurance applicants are correct EXCEPT

    A. The size of the policy being requested generally determines whether an inspection report is ordered by the underwriting department.
    B. Information contained in inspection reports usually is obtained through interviews with employers, neighbors and associates of the proposed insured.
    C. Applicants with unfavorable credit ratings are poor prospects for life insurance.
    D. Inspection reports are requested regardless of the size of the policy.

16. Typically, within how many days must an applicant be notified that a credit report has been requested by the insurer?

    A. Three
    B. Seven
    C. Ten
    D. Thirty

17. Which of the following statements pertaining to a life insurance policy application is CORRECT?

    A. An agent must be very specific when listing an applicant's occupation on an application.
    B. If an applicant's age is shown erroneously on a life insurance application as 28 instead of 29, this could result in a premium quote that is higher than it should be.
    C. The applicant's signature is required on an application, but the agent's signature is not.
    D. An application is not part of the legal contract between insurer and insured, even when it is attached to the policy.

18. Elaine signs an application for a $50,000 life policy, pays the first premium and receives a conditional receipt. If Elaine were killed in an auto accident two days later,

    A. the company could reject the application on the basis that death was accidental
    B. her beneficiary would receive $50,000, if Elaine qualified for the policy as applied for
    C. the premium would be returned to Elaine's family because the policy had not been issued
    D. the insurer could reject the death claim because the underwriting process was never completed

19. Upon issuance of a conditional receipt to an insurance applicant who has paid the insurer an initial premium

    A. the applicant forfeits his or her right to a permanent contract
    B. the applicant eliminates the need to provide the usual application information
    C. the insurance company is conditionally assuming the risk
    D. the insurance company assumes no risk until the policy is issued

20. The primary distinction between the insurability and approval types of conditional receipts is when the

    A. applicant pays the initial premium
    B. coverage goes into effect
    C. medical exam is given
    D. applicant proves insurable

21. Which of the following statements pertaining to a temporary insurance agreement is CORRECT?

    A. It provides protection against death by accident, but not death from natural causes.
    B. It provides temporary coverage until an application is rejected or the policy is issued.
    C. It provides term insurance protection until the policy is converted to permanent insurance.
    D. Coverage begins when the application is signed and the premium is paid, assuming any required medical exam is scheduled within three days.

22. Louise applied for a $40,000 life insurance policy and paid the initial premium, for which she was given a temporary insurance agreement. All of the following statements pertaining to this situation are correct EXCEPT

    A. If Louise took a required medical exam and died four days later from an accidental fall, her beneficiary would receive $40,000.
    B. If Louise died of a heart attack one day after taking the medical exam, the temporary insurance would be payable as a death claim.
    C. If Louise died from an accidental fall a few days before her medical exam, her beneficiary would receive $40,000.
    D. If Louise died of a heart attack one day before taking the medical exam, the temporary insurance would be payable as a death claim.

23. Each application for life insurance requires the signature of all of the following EXCEPT

    A. the proposed insured
    B. the policyowner, if different from the insured
    C. the agent
    D. the beneficiary

24. Upon the issuance of a life insurance policy, an insurable interest must exist between

    A. the applicant and the insured
    B. the applicant and the beneficiary
    C. the insured and the beneficiary
    D. the agent and the applicant

25. All of the following statements pertaining to delivery of a life insurance policy are correct EXCEPT

    A. From a legal standpoint, a policy may be delivered by mail instead of in person if all necessary conditions have been met.

    B. A company issues a policy (the initial premium has been paid) and sends it to the agent for unconditional delivery to the policyowner. This is an example of "constructive delivery."

    C. A company issues a policy (the initial premium has not been paid) and sends it to the agent with instructions not to deliver it unless the applicant is in good health. This is an example of "constructive delivery."

    D. A company issues a policy (the initial premium has been paid) and sends it to the agent for unconditional delivery, but the agent postpones delivery. This is an example of "constructive delivery."

26. Delivering policies in person gives the agent an opportunity to do all of the following EXCEPT

    A. solidify the sale

    B. obtain referrals

    C. build the agent-client relationship and prepare clients for future sales

    D. make last-minute changes to the policy

27. Lawrence signed an application for a life insurance policy on September 2, and took a required medical exam on September 4. He gave the agent a check for the initial premium and received a conditional receipt at the time of application. The agent delivered the policy to him on October 15. Lawrence's insurance protection actually began on

    A. September 2

    B. September 4

    C. October 15

    D. December 31

28. Susan applied for life insurance on November 1, but did not submit a premium payment with the application. She underwent a physical examination on November 10, which she passed, and the results of that exam were forwarded to the insurance company. The policy was issued by the company on November 15, and the agent delivered the policy to Susan on November 17, at which time she paid the first premium. When did Susan's coverage become effective?

    A. November 1

    B. November 10

    C. November 15

    D. November 17

29. Sandra was first interviewed for life insurance on March 25. She applies for preliminary (interim) term insurance on April 10. The issue date of her principal policy is to be July 1 of the same year. The premium for the principal policy will be based on her age as of

    A. January 1

    B. March 25

    C. April 10

    D. July 1

30. Which of the following statements pertaining to preliminary term insurance is CORRECT?

    A. An applicant applies for preliminary term insurance on March 1 and the issue date of the principal policy is June 1 of the same year. The premium for the principal policy will be based on the applicant's age as of March 1.
    B. The premium for the principal policy will be based on the applicant's age as of the issue date of that policy, not of the preliminary policy.
    C. The purpose of this type of insurance is to provide immediate protection for people who cannot afford to purchase permanent life insurance.
    D. Premiums for preliminary term insurance are based on the applicant's age at the end of the interim period.

31. Employees may be classified for group life insurance in all of the following ways EXCEPT

    A. length of service
    B. duties
    C. type of payroll
    D. sex

32. A company has 1,200 eligible employees for its group life insurance program, and the company pays the total premium. How many employees must be insured to initiate the plan?

    A. 600
    B. 900
    C. 1,000
    D. 1,200

33. If a company has 2,000 employees eligible for a noncontributory group life insurance program, how many would be required to participate?

    A. 500
    B. 1,000
    C. 1,500
    D. 2,000

34. All of the following are characteristics of group life insurance EXCEPT

    A. it is usually written without evidence of insurability
    B. minimum participation standards are imposed
    C. each insured in the group receives a policy
    D. the scale of commissions paid on group policies is lower than that on individual policies

35. Which of the following statements with regard to group term life insurance is CORRECT?

    A. Since group term coverage is an employee benefit, employers can select which employees will be covered.
    B. Premiums paid by the employer are tax deductible by the employer and taxable to the employee.
    C. Most group term policies contain a conversion privilege, allowing insureds to convert the coverage to an individual plan if they leave the group.
    D. Group insurance plans must be noncontributory.

36. In writing group insurance, companies use all of the following underwriting guides to guard against adverse risk EXCEPT

    A. medical examinations for prospective insureds who are borderline risks
    B. minimum participation rules
    C. benefits determined by formula
    D. careful group selection

37. All of the following statements about the classification of applicants are correct EXCEPT

    A. a substandard applicant can never be rejected outright by the insurer
    B. applicants who are preferred risks have premium rates that are generally lower than standard rate risks
    C. an individual can be rated as a substandard risk because of a dangerous occupation
    D. a standard applicant fits the insurer's guidelines for policy issue without restrictions

38. An arrangement whereby additional insurance may be purchased at various times without evidence of insurability is known as

    A. free look
    B. constructive delivery
    C. guaranteed issue
    D. loading

39. Who performs the function of risk selection in determining an individual's insurability for policy issue?

    A. Actuary
    B. Agent
    C. Fiduciary
    D. Underwriter

Answers & Rationale

1.   A.   The most common approach to rating insurance applicants is to issue the policy with a higher than standard premium. The higher premium rate may be permanent or temporary, depending on the type of additional risk the applicant poses to the insurer. The third answer choice is a loose variation of the old lien system of rating, which is rarely used today.
QID: 1217

2.   D.   Underwriting is a process by which an insurance company selects, classifies and rates risks. Careful underwriting avoids financial loss for the insurance company.
QID: 1370

3.   C.   Unisex policies offer the same type of coverage for the same premium for men and women. This is a result of legislation that seeks to exclude sex as a factor in premium development.
QID: 1371

4.   B.   All applications for life insurance are not necessarily accompanied by a medical exam; in fact, substantial amounts of life insurance are written by insurers on a nonmedical basis. Part I of the application solicits information about the proposed insured's personal and occupational history. Part II of the application involves the proposed insured's medical history.
QID: 1372

5.   A.   Social Security reports are not sources of insurability information. Inspection reports, the application, the Medical Information Bureau report, credit reports and special questionnaires are important sources of insurability information.
QID: 1373

6.   A.   The record of an applicant's specific injuries should be recorded in the medical section of the application for life insurance. This is the purpose of the medical section.
QID: 1374

7.   B.   If a medical report is required on an applicant, it must be completed by a paramedic or examining physician called a "medical examiner." Medical reports are required when the application for coverage exceeds a certain face amount.
QID: 1375

8.   C.   An applicant's signature is required on the application itself, an aviation questionnaire and authorization form; in other words, forms requiring detailed information from the insured. An agent's report is not given to the applicant and does not require his or her signature.
QID: 1376

9.   B.   Special questionnaires are used to obtain additional information when an extra hazard or risk may be involved (such as skydiving) and to replace the application in unusual cases. A medical report, if required, would be completed by a physician or paramedic, not the agent. An unfavorable credit report could be used to reject an applicant. Investigators do interview individuals who are personally acquainted with the insurance applicant.
QID: 1377

10.   D.   Angela violated the doctrine of concealment since she failed to disclose pertinent, material information on the application. The test of materiality of a concealed fact is whether the company, had it known the fact, would have been influenced in accepting or rejecting a risk.
QID: 1378

11.   B.   All statements made by an insured on an application are considered to be representations, not warranties.
QID: 1379

12.   B.   The Medical Information Bureau (MIB) is a nonprofit central information agency that was established years ago in Boston by a number of life insurance companies to aid in the underwriting process. Its purpose is to provide medical information regarding applicants for insurance. Private hospitals do not have access to the MIB nor do they fund it.
QID: 1380

13.   D.   The Medical Information Bureau (MIB) is a nonprofit central information agency that provides assistance in the underwriting of life insurance. It is not run or accessed by all physicians, nor is data obtained in connection with claims reported to the MIB. Insurance companies report information obtained through underwriting to the MIB.
QID: 1381

14.   B.   To help determine the insurability of applicants, insurance companies normally receive inspection reports on life insurance applicants from national investigative agencies.
QID: 1382

15.   D.   Inspection reports usually are obtained from several knowledgeable sources by insurance companies on applicants who apply for large amounts of life insurance. An applicant's poor credit rating can mean unreliable premium payments, causing the insurance company to lose money.
QID: 1383

16.   A.   With the Fair Credit Reporting Act, applicants must be notified (usually within three days) that the credit report has been requested by the insurer. The insurer must also notify the applicant that he or she can request disclosure of the nature and scope of the investigation.
QID: 1384

17.   A.   An agent must be very specific when listing an applicant's occupation and duties on the application because of the insurer's need to evaluate job hazards that may affect insurability. An applicant whose age is erroneously shown to be younger than his or her actual age will receive a premium quote that is lower than it should be. Both the applicant and agent must sign the application. The application is considered part of the legal contract when it is attached to the insurance policy.
QID: 1385

18.   B.   Provided the applicant qualifies for coverage, he or she is immediately insured at the time of application upon paying an initial premium and receiving a conditional receipt.
QID: 1386

19.   C.   When the company issues a conditional receipt, it is initiating a conditional contract, which means it is providing early coverage and assuming the risk. The condition upon which the contract is issued is the applicant's qualification for the policy he or she applied for.
QID: 1387

20.   B.   A conditional receipt indicates that certain conditions must be met in order for the insurance coverage to go into effect. The approval receipt is more restrictive because coverage is effective only after the policy is approved.
QID: 1388

21.   B.   A temporary insurance agreement is just that temporary coverage until an application is rejected or the policy is issued.
QID: 1389

22.   D.   If a medical exam is required, the temporary insurance agreement would not go into effect until the applicant takes the medical exam.
QID: 1390

23.   D.   Each application for life insurance requires the signature of the insured, the policyowner (if different from the insured) and the agent.
QID: 1391

24.   A.   Upon the issuance of a life insurance policy, the applicant must have an insurable interest in the life of the individual to be insured. While an insurable interest must exist at the time of issuance, it need not exist at the time of the insured's death.
QID: 1392

25.   C.   Policy delivery may be accomplished without physically delivering the policy into the policyowner's possession. For instance, "constructive delivery" is accomplished if the com-

pany turns over the policy to the insured's agent. Mailing the policy to the agent for unconditional delivery to the policy owner also is constructive delivery. If the company places a condition on the delivery, such as the policy owner being in good health, there is no constructive delivery.
QID: 1393

26. D. Delivering policies in person gives an agent the opportunity to solidify the sale, obtain referrals and prepare clients for future sales. An agent cannot make any last-minute changes to the policy after it has been issued, unless it is done so according to strict compliance with state and insurance company regulations.
QID: 1394

27. B. When a conditional receipt is used, the insurer is considered to have made an offer of coverage, conditioned upon the applicant's insurability. The insurance becomes effective as of the date of the medical exam, assuming the applicant meets the underwriting criteria and is insurable. The date the policy is actually delivered to the insured is immaterial.
QID: 1395

28. D. In situations where the applicant does not submit a premium with the application, the issuance of the policy (if he or she is found to be insurable) and its delivery to the applicant constitute the contractual offer. The applicant accepts the company's offer when the first premium is paid, and it is on that date that the contract becomes effective.
QID: 1396

29. D. Under the conditions of preliminary term insurance, the premium for the principal policy will be based on the applicant's age as of the issue date of that policy.
QID: 1397

30. B. The premium for the principal policy will be based on the insured's attained age as of the issue date of the principal policy. By using preliminary term insurance, the applicant can be

insured without delay and still postpone payment of premium on the principal policy for one or more months for added convenience.
QID: 1398

31. D. Employees may be classified for group life insurance in many ways, such as length of service, duties and type of payroll, except according to sex.
QID: 1399

32. D. If a group life insurance plan is noncontributory, 100 percent of eligible persons must be insured.
QID: 1400

33. D. If a group life insurance plan is noncontributory, 100 percent of eligible persons must be insured.
QID: 1401

34. C. A distinguishing characteristic of group life insurance is its use of a master contract that sets forth the terms and conditions between the insurance company and the policyowner, which is the employer. Those covered by the contract—the employees—do not receive individual policies and are not parties to the contract. Each insured instead receives a certificate of insurance.
QID: 1402

35. C. Employers who provide group term life insurance plans cannot discriminatively limit participation nor can they arrange the plans to favor key employees. Any premiums paid by the employer are not considered taxable income to the covered employee, though they are deductible by the employer. Group plans may be contributory or noncontributory.
QID: 1403

36. A. Medical examinations for borderline risks are not used in underwriting group insurance to guard against adverse selection.
QID: 1404

37. A. A substandard risk is one below the insurer's standard or average risk guidelines. Some substandard applicants are rejected outright; others will be accepted for coverage but with an increase in their policy premium or an exclusion for specified coverage.
QID: 1405

38. C. An arrangement whereby additional insurance may be purchased at various times without evidence of insurability is known as guaranteed issue.
QID: 1406

39. D. The process of determining who so qualified to purchase life insurance and who is not is called risk selection. This task is performed by insurance company underwriters.
QID: 3340

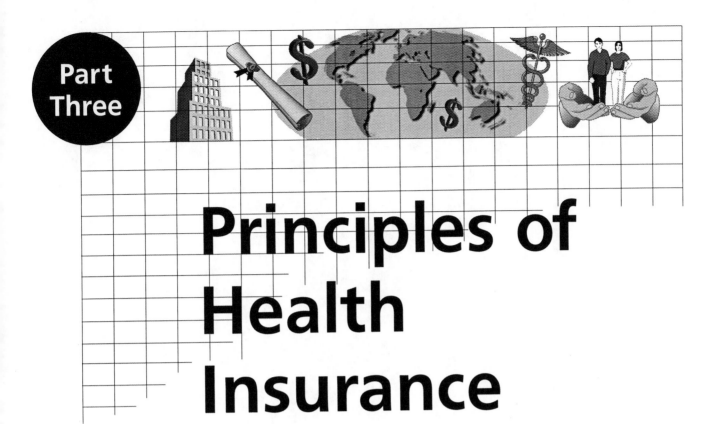

Part Three

Principles of Health Insurance

Nature of Accident and Health Insurance

1. The beneficiary of an accidental death and dismemberment (AD&D) policy receives $25,000 after the insured is killed in an auto accident. The $25,000 death benefit otherwise could be identified as the policy's

   A. primary benefit
   B. principal sum
   C. maximum figure
   D. capital sum

2. The amount paid for the accidental loss of sight or dismemberment under an AD&D policy is known as the policy's

   A. primary sum
   B. dismemberment sum
   C. capital sum
   D. secondary sum

3. All of the following are classified as a type of accident and sickness insurance coverage EXCEPT

   A. Disability income insurance
   B. Medical expense insurance
   C. Dental insurance
   D. Variable annuity

4. Which of the following statements is CORRECT?

   A. Disability income insurance reimburses the insured for medical care, hospital care and related services for disabled insureds.
   B. Medical expense insurance provides periodic payments to the insured when he or she is unable to work due to sickness or injury.
   C. Long-term care insurance provides benefits to the insured for hospital care immediately following a surgical procedure.
   D. Accidental death insurance provides a stated lump-sum benefit in the event of accidental death.

5. Which of the following types of health insurance coverage is always available under a group basis?

   A. Disability income
   B. Medical expense
   C. Accidental death and dismemberment
   D. Maternity care

6. All of the following types of health insurance coverage can be written on an individual basis EXCEPT

    A. Disability income
    B. Medical expense
    C. Accidental death and dismemberment
    D. Social Security

7. Agnes purchases a round-trip travel accident policy at the airport before leaving on a business trip. Her policy would be which type of insurance?

    A. Limited risk
    B. Business overhead expense
    C. Credit accident and health
    D. Industrial health

8. All of the following types of companies underwrite health insurance EXCEPT

    A. life insurance companies
    B. casualty insurance companies
    C. mono-line companies
    D. annuity companies

9. When available, dental and vision care coverages generally are issued in what type of health insurance policies?

    A. Group
    B. Blanket
    C. Individual
    D. Franchise

10. State-sponsored programs that generally provide nonoccupational disability coverage are known as

    A. income security insurance
    B. statutory disability plans
    C. worker's insurance
    D. compensation guaranty programs

11. Medicare is an example of

    A. commercial insurance
    B. casualty insurance
    C. debt insurance
    D. social insurance

12. For group health insurance, employees may be classified in all of the following ways EXCEPT by

    A. type of payroll
    B. duties
    C. length of service
    D. age

13. All of the following are considered service providers EXCEPT

    A. preferred provider organization
    B. commercial insurance company
    C. health maintenance organization
    D. Blue Cross/Blue Shield

14. All of the following statements regarding Blue Cross and Blue Shield are correct EXCEPT

    A. they are nonprofit health care membership groups
    B. they are organized on a geographic basis
    C. they can declare dividends and distribute earnings to enrollees
    D. they offer health-care coverage on both an individual and a group basis

15. Which of the following accurately describes the service approach used by Blue Cross and Blue Shield?

    A. Blue Shield plans provide prepayment coverage for hospital expenses; Blue Cross plans provide prepayment coverage for medical and surgical services.
    B. Both Blue Cross and Blue Shield reimburse their subscribers for covered medical and hospital expenses.
    C. Blue Cross and Blue Shield are for-profit organizations run by insurance companies.
    D. Both Blue Cross and Blue Shield plans do not reimburse for covered expenses, but pay health care providers directly.

16. All of the following statements apply to Blue Cross and/or Blue Shield EXCEPT

   A. both are voluntary, nonprofit organizations T
   B. under a Blue Cross hospital plan, the insured is billed directly for covered services received in a member hospital F
   C. both Blue Cross and Blue Shield have contractual arrangements with hospitals and participating physicians as to rate or fee schedules
   D. Blue Cross plans are designed primarily to provide hospital benefits

17. Which of the following statements pertaining to health maintenance organizations (HMOs) is CORRECT? T

   A. An insurance company that markets group health insurance also is known as an HMO. F
   B. If a person joins an HMO and undergoes a physical examination, he or she will be billed for the exam and each subsequent medical service as it is performed. F
   C. HMOs are funded by the federal government, and eligibility is determined by the income levels of the participants. F
   D. An HMO offers comprehensive services on a prepaid basis to its subscribing members. T

18. Which of the following statements regarding persons participating in a HMO is CORRECT?

   A. They pay for health care services as they are incurred. F
   B. They negotiate health care service fees with contracted HMO providers. F
   C. They pay a fixed periodic fee whether or not health care services are used. F
   D. They pay for health care services as they are incurred, at a rate discounted for the HMO.

19. Which of the following statements concerning HMOs is CORRECT? T

   A. They place special emphasis on preventive health care. T
   B. Participants pay a one-time, fixed fee in advance for health-care services. F
   C. HMOs generally are owned by life insurance companies. F
   D. They primarily provide emergency medical treatment for their members. F

20. The type of HMO that employs its own physicians and that requires its members to use these physicians is known as a(n)

   A. closed-panel HMO
   B. open-panel HMO
   C. nonparticipating HMO
   D. general HMO

21. All of the following statements about preferred provider organizations are correct EXCEPT F

   A. they operate on a fee-for-service rendered basis T
   B. they offer health care services to their members at discounted rates that are negotiated in advance T
   C. they offer health care coverage to low-income individuals
   D. physicians who are part of a PPO are in private practice T

22. All of the following groups may contract with PPOs EXCEPT

   A. employers
   B. insurance companies
   C. health insurance benefit providers
   D. government programs

23. Health policies classified as "nonoccupational" normally provide coverage for

   A. losses due to sickness or accidents that are not work-related
   B. persons in nonhazardous jobs
   C. losses both on and off the job
   D. sickness but not for accidental injuries

24. Workers' compensation covers income loss resulting from

    A. work-related disabilities
    B. any accidental injury
    C. unemployment
    D. sickness

25. All of the following are examples of health plan administrators EXCEPT

    A. HMO
    B. ASO
    C. TPA
    D. Medicare

26. All of the following statements regarding multiple-employer trusts (METs) are correct EXCEPT

    A. they are established to provide group benefits to employers within a specific industry, such as construction
    B. an employer desiring coverage for its employees from a MET must subscribe by becoming a member of the trust
    C. METs provide coverage only on a self-funded basis
    D. METs are most typically used by smaller employers

27. Which of the following plans uses an outside, noninsurance organization to handle the paperwork for a self-insurance plan?

    A. multiple employer trust (MET)
    B. administrative-services-only (ASO) plan
    C. third-party administrator (TPA) plan
    D. minimum premium plan (MPP)

28. A group in which a number of employers pool their risks and self-insure is called a

    A. multiple employer trust (MET)
    B. multiple administrative plan (MAP)
    C. multiple employer welfare arrangement (MEWA)
    D. combined risk plan (CRP)

29. When evaluating health carriers, all of the following are valid considerations EXCEPT

    A. reimbursement procedures
    B. services provided
    C. contractual arrangements
    D. location of their headquarters

30. Who are the owners of a mutual insurance company?

    A. Stockholders
    B. Directors
    C. Employers
    D. Policyowners

31. Jim is a professional pilot who is testing an experimental new plane. He purchases a policy which provides benefits if accidental death or injury results while flying that plane. This type of policy is a

    A. limited risk policy
    B. special risk policy
    C. travel accident policy
    D. specific accident policy

32. Stan intentionally jumped out a tree after retrieving a kite instead of using a ladder. He severely injured his arm, which later had to be amputated. His AD&D policy paid no benefits. Stan's policy bases its benefit payments on

    A. accidental means
    B. intentional means
    C. accidental results
    D. accidental means and results

Answers & Rationale

1.   B.   The death benefit under an AD&D policy is known as the "principal sum."
QID: 1444

2.   C.   The benefit paid under an AD&D policy for the accidental loss of sight or for dismemberment is known as the "capital sum."
QID: 1445

3.   D.   Disability income, medical expense and dental insurance represent major categories of accident and sickness insurance. Within these categories is a wide range of coverages. A variable annuity is a type of contract that provides a varying income for a particular lifetime or other specified period.
QID: 1446

4.   D.   Disability income insurance pays a periodic benefit to the insured as a supplement to salary when he or she is disabled and unable to work because of sickness or accident. Medical expense insurance reimburses the insured for actual expenses incurred for medical and hospital care and related services. Long-term care insurance provides benefits to cover care for an extended period of time usually in a nursing home, an adult care center or in the home.
QID: 1447

5.   D.   Disability income, medical expense and AD&D insurance can all be written on both an individual and a group basis. It is a federal regulation, however, that all group plans offer maternity care. Most individual plans do not offer maternity benefits.
QID: 1448

6.   D.   Disability income, medical expense and AD&D insurance can all be written on an individual basis. Social Security is a federally administered program that provides retirement, death and disability benefits for qualified workers.
QID: 1449

7.   A.   Limited risk policies are another type of AD&D coverage that provide protection against accidental death or dismemberment only in the event of certain specified accidents, such as a death or injury resulting from an aviation accident during a specified trip.
QID: 1450

8.   D.   Health insurance may be written by a life insurance company, a casualty insurance company, or a mono-line firm that specializes in medical expense and disability insurance. Annuity companies write contracts that provide life benefits for the insured while he or she is alive.
QID: 1451

9.   A.   Dental and vision care coverages are normally found in group health insurance policies. They are seldom written on an individual basis.
QID: 1452

10.   B.   State-sponsored programs that generally provide nonoccupational disability coverage are known as statutory disability programs. They are required in only a few states.
QID: 1453

11.   D.   Medicare is an example of a social insurance program, instituted by the federal government.
QID: 1454

12.   D.   For group insurance, employees may be classified by type of payroll, duties or length of service. There can be no discrimination as to age, sex or race.
QID: 1455

13.   B.   Service providers include HMOs, PPOs and Blue Cross/Blue Shield organizations. They are characterized by providing their members with health care services. In contrast, commercial insurers reimburse their policyowners for health care costs.
QID: 1456

14. C. All of the statements are true except the third answer choice. Blue Cross and Blue Shield plans are generally organized as nonprofit entities, and as such do not amass profits or declare dividends.
QID: 1457

15. D. Blue Cross and Blue Shield are not-for-profit health care service organizations. Blue Shield plans provide prepayment coverage for medical and surgical expenses, while Blue Cross plans provide prepayment coverage for hospital expenses. Both Blue Cross and Blue Shield plans operate under the service approach which does not involve reimbursement for covered expenses but rather a guarantee that covered services will be provided without charge to their subscribers.
QID: 1458

16. B. Under a Blue Cross Hospital Plan, the insured is billed only for services not covered by the plan. Payments for standard services are made by Blue Cross/Blue Shield directly to the hospital.
QID: 1459

17. D. An insurance company may sponsor an HMO or assist an HMO by providing contractual services. Many HMOs are independent. HMO members pay fixed periodic fees whether or not they use the HMO services; they are not subsequently charged for medical services performed.
QID: 1460

18. C. Persons participating in an HMO pay a fixed periodic fee in advance for services performed by participating physicians and hospitals. This fee is payable, whether or not the participant uses any health care service.
QID: 1461

19. A. HMOs place special emphasis on preventive health care. Subscribers pay a fixed, periodic fee for the broad range of health care services provided.
QID: 1462

20. A. An HMO that employs its own physicians and requires members to use these physicians is known as a "closed-panel HMO." An open-panel HMO, on the other hand, maintains an association of participating physicians, who accept non-HMO patients as well as HMO subscribers. Subscribers choose from among the physicians on the list.
QID: 1463

21. C. The PPO (preferred provider organization) is similar to an HMO, but members pay for services as they are provided at rates that have been discounted in advance for the PPO. Physicians offering their services through a PPO are in private practice.
QID: 1464

22. D. All answer choices but the last one are typical groups that contract with PPOs. While these groups do not mandate that individual members must use the PPO, a reduced benefit is typical if they do not. For instance, members may pay a $100 deductible if they use PPO services and a $500 deductible if they go outside the PPO for health care services.
QID: 1465

23. A. Policies classified as nonoccupational normally provide coverage for losses due to sickness or accidents that are not work related.
QID: 1466

24. A. Workers' compensation covers income loss resulting from work-related disabilities. It does not cover injuries unrelated to a person's employment. It does not provide unemployment benefits.
QID: 1467

25. D. Every entity listed is a health plan administrator. HMOs (Health Maintenance Organizations) are commercial health organizations offering health care services to subscribers. ASOs (Administrative Services Only plans) are any groups—including insurance companies—that handle the administration of claims, benefits and other administrative functions for self-insured groups. TPAs (Third-Party Administrators) are

those ASOs that are not insurance companies. Medicare is a federally funded program that provides insurance for hospital and medical expenses.
QID: 1468

26. C. All of the statements are true, except the third answer choice. METs can provide benefits on a self-funded basis or they can add benefits through a contract issued by an insurance company. In the latter case, the trust itself, rather than the subscribing employers, is the master contract holder.
QID: 1469

27. C. An outside, noninsurance organization (a "third party") that handles the paperwork for a self-insurance plan is called a third-party administrator (TPA).
QID: 1470

28. C. In a MEWA, a number of employers pool their risks and self-insure, rather than obtain coverage from an insurance company.
QID: 1471

29. D. Important distinctions can be made among health carriers in the areas of reimbursement procedures, contractual arrangements and services provided. Where the carriers' business officers are located is not considered an important factor.
QID: 1472

30. D. Every policyowner of a mutual insurance company, by virtue of his or her policy, also owns a share of the insurance company. A mutual insurance company has no capital stock and usually issues participating policies.
QID: 1473

31. B. Jim purchased a special risk policy. A special risk policy covers unusual hazards normally not covered under ordinary accident and health insurance.
QID: 3341

32. A. Stan's AD&D policy bases its benefit payments on accidental means. This type of policy requires that both the cause and the result of an accident be unintentional. Policies that use the accidental results definition stipulate that only the injury resulting from an accident must be unintentional.
QID: 3342

12

Senior Health Insurance Plans

1. Currently, the largest share of the cost of nursing home care for the elderly is paid for by
   A. Medicare and Medicare supplement policies
   B. Medicaid
   C. nursing home residents and their families
   D. medical insurance

2. Which of these statements regarding Medicare is CORRECT?
   A. Medicare Part B Supplement Medicare Insurance (SMI) is voluntary.
   B. Under Medicare Part B, payments for physicians' services are unlimited.
   C. Medicare recipients are billed for their Medicare Part A premiums on a semiannual basis.
   D. Medicare Part A Hospital Insurance (HI) carries no deductible.

3. Under Medicare Part A, the participant must pay his or her deductible
   A. annually
   B. once per benefit period
   C. monthly
   D. twice per benefit period

4. Medicare supplement (Medigap) policies are designed to pay
   A. medical costs associated with extended custodial (nursing home) care
   B. most or all of Medicare's deductibles
   C. benefits provided under Medicare Part A
   D. benefits to those who cannot afford Medicare Part B coverage

5. Under Medicare Part B, the participant must pay
   A. 20 percent of covered charges above the deductible
   B. a per benefit deductible
   C. 80 percent of covered charges above the deductible
   D. a yearly premium

6. Lynn is insured under Medicare Part A and enters the hospital for surgery. Assuming that Lynn has not yet tapped into her lifetime reserve, what is the maximum number of days that Medicare will pay for her hospital bills?
   A. 60
   B. 90
   C. 120
   D. 150

7. What are the sources of funding for Medicare Parts A and B?

   A. Social Security payroll taxes for Part A, and participants' contributions and general revenues for Part B
   B. Participants' contributions for Part A, and Social Security payroll taxes for Part B
   C. Federal tax revenue for Part A, and U.S. Savings Bonds for Part B
   D. States' general revenue funds for Part A, and states' general obligation bonds for Part B

8. Charles signs up for Medicare Part B on March 21 during the open enrollment period. His coverage will become effective

   A. March 21
   B. April 1
   C. June 30
   D. July 1

9. Which of the following is covered by Medicare?

   A. x-rays
   B. eyeglasses
   C. immunizations
   D. foot care

10. To be eligible for Medicare's nursing home benefit, the claimant must first do all of the following EXCEPT

   A. spend at least three days in a hospital
   B. enter a Medicare-certified skilled nursing facility
   C. have a physician certify that skilled care is required
   D. meet acceptable income limits

11. Which of the following statements pertaining to Medicare is CORRECT?

   A. Bob is covered under Medicare Part B. He submitted a total of $1,100 of approved medical charges to Medicare after paying the required deductible. Of that total, Bob must pay $880.
   B. Each individual covered by Medicare Part A is allowed one 90-day benefit period per year.
   C. For the first 90 days of hospitalization, Medicare Part A pays 100 percent of all covered services, except for an initial deductible.
   D. Medicare Part A is automatically provided when a qualified individual applies for Social Security benefits.

12. People age 65 or older who enroll in Medicare Part B may also select Medigap coverage during a(n)

   A. open enrollment period
   B. free-look period
   C. grace period
   D. free-enrollment period

13. What is the maximum number of days of skilled nursing facility care for which Medicare will pay

   A. 25
   B. 60
   C. 75
   D. 100

14. The "core policy" (Plan A) developed by the NAIC as a standard Medicare supplement policy includes all of the following EXCEPT

   A. coverage for Part A copayment amounts
   B. the first three pints of blood each year
   C. the 20 percent Part B coinsurance amounts for Medicare-approved services
   D. foreign travel emergency care

15. Individuals claiming a need for Medicaid must prove that they cannot pay for their own nursing home care. In addition, the potential recipient must

 A. be at least 70 years old
 B. need the type of care that is provided only in a nursing home
 C. be on Social Security
 D. be a long-term care insurance policy-owner

16. Which of the following is a common benefit trigger for a long-term care policy?

 A. Prior hospitalization
 B. Cognitive or mental impairment
 C. Retirement
 D. Inability to operate a motor vehicle

17. Which of the following types of care is described as "a broad range of medical, personal and environmental services designed to assist individuals who have lost their ability to remain completely independent in the community?"

 A. In-house care
 B. Chronic care
 C. Long-term care
 D. Specified care

18. Skilled nursing care differs from intermediate care in which of the following ways?

 A. Skilled nursing care must be performed by skilled medical professionals whereas intermediate care does not require medical training.
 B. Skilled care must be available 24 hours a day while intermediate care is daily, but not 24-hour, care.
 C. Skilled care is typically given in a nursing home, while intermediate care is usually given at home.
 D. Skilled care encompasses rehabilitation, while intermediate care is for meeting daily personal needs, such as bathing and dressing.

19. All of the following conditions are typically covered in a long-term insurance policy EXCEPT

 A. Alzheimer's disease
 B. senile dementia
 C. alcohol dependency
 D. Parkinson's disease

20. Which of the following statements with respect to the lifetime reserve of hospital coverage for Medicare patients is CORRECT?

 A. Tapping into the reserve results in a lower daily copayment.
 B. The reserve does not renew with a new benefit period.
 C. The reserve may be replenished if the patient reenters a hospital after a benefit period ends and pays a new deductible.
 D. If a patient exhausts the reserve, he or she must pay a higher copayment.

21. What benefits does Medicare provide for treatment in a skilled nursing care facility after 100 days?

 A. Coverage for diagnostic services and medical supplies only
 B. Reduced coverage with a higher copayment from the insured
 C. Coverage for physical and occupational therapy only
 D. None

22. All of the following are offered to Medicare beneficiaries by the Medicare+Choice Program EXCEPT

 A. Health maintenance organizations (HMOs)
 B. Preferred provider organizations (PPOs)
 C. Provider-sponsored organizations (PSOs)
 D. Medicaid

23. Long-term care coverage may consist of all of the following EXCEPT

    A. institutional care
    B. home-based care
    C. community care
    D. surgical care

24. The average minimum age at which a person can purchase a long-term care insurance policy is

    A. 40
    B. 50
    C. 65
    D. 70

25. A long-term care insurance policy must contain which of the following provisions?

    A. Guaranteed renewability
    B. Coverage for drug and alcohol dependency
    C. Probationary period of no longer than 180 days
    D. Coverage for conditions that result from war

26. How long a period of institutionalization can be required before home health care benefits are available in a long-term care policy?

    A. 30 days
    B. 60 days
    C. 90 days
    D. 365 days

27. A Medicare+Choice Medical Savings Account consists of a(n)

    A. high deductible insurance policy and a savings account
    B. private fee-for-service plan and a savings account
    C. HMO and a separate account
    D. PPO and a separate account

28. Long-term care insurance provides care for an extended period of time that usually exceeds how many days?

    A. 30
    B. 60
    C. 90
    D. 120

29. If Sue's daily benefit amount under her long-term care policy is $150 a day and her nursing home charges $100 a day

    A. the insurance company will only pay $100, the cost of her nursing home care
    B. the insurance company will pay $100 a day to the nursing home and will apply the extra $50 to future premiums
    C. the insurance company will pay the full $150 a day
    D. the insurance company will pay the full $150 a day but will require Sue to use the extra $50 to pay for future premiums

30. All of the following statements about Medicare supplement (Medigap) policies are correct EXCEPT

    A. Medigap policies supplement Medicare benefits.
    B. Medigap policies cover the cost of extended nursing home care.
    C. Medigap policies pay most, if not all, Medicare deductibles and copayments.
    D. Medigap policies pay for some health care services not covered by Medicare.

Answers & Rationale

1.   C.   Most of the cost of nursing home care is paid by the nursing home resident or shifted to his or her family. The average cost of a nursing home stay is between $40,000 and $50,000 per year.
QID: 1474

2.   A.   Medicare coverage has two distinct parts Hospital Insurance (Part A) and Medical Insurance (Part B). Medicare Part B is voluntary and may be elected or rejected as the recipient wishes.
QID: 1475

3.   B.   For Medicare Part A, the participant must pay his or her deductible once per benefit period. A benefit period starts when a patient enters the hospital and ends when the patient has been out of the hospital for 60 consecutive days. Once 60 days have passed, any new hospital admission is considered to be the start of a new benefit period. Thus, if a patient reenters a hospital after a benefit period ends, a new deductible is required and the 90-day hospital coverage period is renewed.
QID: 1476

4.   B.   Medicare supplement insurance or Medigap policies are designed to pick up coverage where Medicare leaves off. The purpose of these policies is to supplement Medicare's benefits by paying most, if not all, coinsurance amounts and deductibles and paying for some health care services not covered by Medicare, such as outpatient prescription drugs. They do not cover the cost of extended nursing home care.
QID: 1477

5.   A.   Part B participants are required to pay a monthly premium and are responsible for an annual deductible. After the deductible, Part B will pay 80 percent of covered expenses, subject to Medicare's standards for reasonable charges.
QID: 1478

6.   D.   After an initial deductible, Medicare pays for all covered hospital charges for the first 60 days of hospitalization. The next 30 days are also covered, but the patient will be required to "co-pay" a certain daily amount. If, after these first 90 days the patient is still hospitalized, he or she can tap into a lifetime reserve of an additional 60 days, paying a higher level of daily co-payments. Consequently, a patient who has not yet tapped into the lifetime reserve days could have up to 150 days of Medicare coverage for one hospital stay.
QID: 1479

7.   A.   Medicare Part A is financed by tax funds provided through the Social Security program. Part B is financed by participants' contributions and tax revenues, as it is a voluntary medical insurance program.
QID: 1480

8.   D.   Medicare Part B coverage for those who sign on during the open enrollment period always becomes effective the following July 1.
QID: 1481

9.   A.   Medicare Part B covers x-rays and other diagnostic tests.
QID: 1482

10.   D.   Medicare nursing home benefits are available only if the following three conditions are met The patient must have been hospitalized for at least three days before entering the nursing home and admittance to the nursing home must be within 30 days of discharge from the hospital; a doctor must certify that skilled nursing is required; and the services must be provided by a Medicare-certified skilled nursing facility.
QID: 1483

11.   D.   Medicare Part A is available when an individual turns 65 and is automatically provided when he or she applies for Social Security benefits. Medicare Part B pays 80 percent of medical expenses after the insured pays the deductible.
QID: 1484

12. A. People age 65 or older who enroll in Medicare Part B are afforded a six-month open enrollment period for purchasing Medigap insurance coverage. The coverage becomes effective the following July 1.
QID: 1485

13. D. Part A covers the costs of care in a skilled nursing facility as long as the patient was first hospitalized for three consecutive days. Medicare will cover treatment in a skilled nursing facility in full for the first 20 days. From the 21st to the 100th day, the patient must pay a daily copayment (up to $97 per day in 2000). There are no Medicare benefits provided for treatment in a skilled nursing facility beyond 100
QID: 1486

14. D. This plan includes coverage for Part A copayment amounts; 365 additional (lifetime) days of Medicare-eligible expenses once the Medicare lifetime reserve days are exhausted; the 20 percent Part B copayment amounts (for Medicare-approved services); and the first three pints of blood each year. At a minimum, all Medicare supplement policies must contain these "core" benefits.
QID: 1487

15. B. To qualify for Medicaid nursing home benefits, the recipient must be at least 65 years old, blind or disabled; be a U.S. citizen or permanent resident alien; need the type of care that is provided in a nursing home; and meet certain asset and income tests.
QID: 1488

16. B. A benefit trigger is an event or condition that must occur before policy benefits become payable. Under the Health Insurance Portability and Accountability Act of 1996 (HIPAA), the individual must be diagnosed as "chronically ill" to trigger benefits; prior hospitalization can no longer be used as a trigger. Diagnosis of "chronically ill" can be based on two conditions physical or cognitive illness. The physical diagnosis of a chronically ill individual is one who has been certified as being unable to perform at least two

activities of daily living (ADLs), which are defined as eating, toileting, transferring (walking), bathing, dressing and continence. A long-term care policy must take into account at least five of these ADLs. An individual would also be considered chronically ill if he or she requires substantial supervision to protect his or her health or safety because of severe cognitive impairment, and the condition was certified within the previous 12 months.
QID: 1489

17. C. Long-term care (LTC) refers to care provided for an extended period of time, normally more than 90 days. Depending on the severity of the impairment, assistance may be given at home, at an adult care center or in a nursing home.
QID: 1490

18. B. Unlike intermediate care, skilled nursing care is continuous around-the-clock care provided by licensed medical professionals under the direct supervision of a physician. It is usually administered in nursing homes. Intermediate care is provided by registered nurses, licensed practical nurses and nurse's aides under the supervision of a physician. Intermediate care is provided in nursing homes for stable medical conditions that require daily, but not 24-hour, supervision.
QID: 1491

19. C. Most LTC insurance policies exclude coverage for drug and alcohol dependency, acts of war, self-inflicted injuries and nonorganic mental conditions. Organic cognitive disorders, such as Alzheimer's disease, senile dementia and Parkinson's disease, are almost always included.
QID: 1492

20. B. The lifetime reserve is an additional 60 days of coverage on top of the 90-day benefit period Medicare provides for hospitalization. A patient who is hospitalized for longer than 90 days can tap into the 60-day reserve. This reserve is a one-time benefit; it is not replenished with a new benefit period. Tapping into the reserve will require a higher copayment from the patient. If a

patient is hospitalized beyond the 60th lifetime reserve day, thus exhausting the reserve, he or she will be responsible for all hospital charges.
QID: 1493

21. D. Medicare does not pay benefits for treatment in a skilled nursing care facility beyond 100 days.
QID: 1494

22. D. The Medicare+Choice Program, implemented after December 31, 1999, gives Medicare beneficiaries a variety of alternatives from which to obtain Medicare-covered services. Medicare participants are also able to take advantage of tax-free medical savings accounts (Medicare+Choice MSAs) for routine medical bills and a government-funded high-deductible Medicare+Choice MSA health plan (MSA plan) for catastrophic expenses. The program also offers a combination of private fee-for-service health plans and self-funding, and private contracts with doctors for particular services. Medicaid offers assistance with medical costs to low-income individuals.
QID: 1495

23. D. Long-term care insurance typically provides coverage for skilled nursing care, intermediate nursing care, custodial care, home health care, adult day care, respite care and continuing care.
QID: 1496

24. B. Many long-term care policies set a minimum age for the purchase of such a policy, with the average limit at 50 years. They also typically set age limits for issuance of a policy, with the average at about 79. Some newer policies can be sold to people as old as age 89.
QID: 1497

25. A. As a result of the 1996 Health Insurance Portability and Accountability Act (HIPAA), all long-term care policies sold today must be guaranteed renewable. The insurer cannot cancel the policy and must renew coverage each year, as long as the insured pays the premiums.
QID: 1498

26. A. If a long-term care policy requires that the insured be institutionalized before qualifying for home health care benefits, the period of required institutionalization cannot be longer than 30 days.
QID: 1499

27. A. A Medicare+Choice Medical Savings Account consists of two parts a high deductible insurance policy and a savings account. The policy pays for at least all Medicare-covered items and services after an enrollee meets the annual deductible. Medicare pays the premium for the policy and deposits the difference between the premium and the fixed amount Medicare allots for each Medicare+Choice enrollee in the individual's savings account.
QID: 3343

28. C. Although care may be provided for short periods of time while a patient is recuperating from an accident or illness, long-term care refers to care provided for an extended period of time, normally more than 90 days.
QID: 3344

29. C. Most long-term care policies will pay the insured a fixed dollar amount for each day he or she receives the kind of care the policy covers, regardless of what the care costs. Because Sue's daily benefit amount is $150 per day, her insurance company will pay the full $150 per day, even though her nursing home only charges $100 a day. She can decide what to do with the remaining funds.
QID: 3345

30. B. Medigap policies are designed to supplement Medicare's benefits by paying most deductibles and copayments as well as some health services not covered by Medicare. Medigap policies do not cover the cost of extended nursing home care.
QID: 3346

13

Health Insurance Policy Provisions

1. An insurer may change the wording of a uniform policy provision in its health insurance policies ONLY if the

   A. company's board of directors approves the change
   B. modified provision is not less favorable to the insurer
   C. policyowners agree in writing to the change
   D. modified provision is not less favorable to the insured or beneficiaries

2. Which of the following is usually included in an individual health insurance contract?

   A. types of losses associated with preexisting conditions
   B. situations involving deliberate acts of the insured, such as self-inflicted injuries
   C. losses that are covered by workers' compensation
   D. injuries due to an accident

3. All of the following are required provisions for accident and health policies EXCEPT

   A. proof of loss
   B. entire contract and changes
   C. change of beneficiary
   D. misstatement of age

4. Children of the insured are eligible for health insurance coverage under a family policy until they attain age 19 or, if they remain in school, age

   A. 20
   B. 21
   C. 22
   D. 23

5. All of the following are required provisions in health insurance policies EXCEPT

   A. notice of claim
   B. grace period
   C. entire contract
   D. change of occupation

6. The entire contract in health insurance includes all of the following EXCEPT

   A. the policy itself
   B. endorsements to the policy
   C. riders attached to the policy
   D. buyer's guide

7. When it is used, the time limit on certain defenses provision in a health insurance policy provides that the policy cannot be contested nor claims denied after two (or three) years EXCEPT for

   A. nonpayment of premiums
   B. mental incompetence of the insured
   C. fraudulent statements in the application
   D. incomplete policy records

8. All of the following statements pertaining to the grace period and reinstatement provisions in health insurance policies are correct EXCEPT

   A. Craig's health policy has a grace period of 31 days. He had a premium come due June 15 while he was on vacation. He returned home July 7 and mailed his premium the next day. His policy would have remained in force.
   B. Warren's medical expense policy was reinstated on September 30 and he became ill and entered the hospital on October 5. His hospital expense will not be paid by the insurer.
   C. Under a health policy's reinstatement terms, insured losses from accidental injuries and sicknesses are covered immediately after reinstatement.
   D. States may require grace periods of seven, ten or 31 days, depending on the mode of premium payment or term of insurance.

9. Which of the following is the usual grace period for a semi-annual premium policy?

   A. 7 days
   B. 20 days
   C. 31 days
   D. 60 days

10. Insured losses are covered immediately after a health policy is reinstated when

    A. the losses result from accidental injuries
    B. all back premiums have been paid
    C. hospitalization is required
    D. claim forms are submitted with proof of loss

11. All of the following statements pertaining to health insurance policy notice of claims and claim forms provisions are correct EXCEPT

    A. Charlotte is injured January 5. Later, she wishes to file a policy claim for expenses incurred in connection with the injury. Generally, she would be required to submit a notice of claim to the company by February 5.
    B. Rex, the insured in a disability income policy, has been totally disabled and receiving benefits for 25 months. The notice of claims provision in his policy requires that he submit proof of loss every six
    C. Gail submits notice of claim to her insurance company after she becomes totally disabled. The company is to supply a claims form to her within 15 days.
    D. Furnishing claim forms is the responsibility of the insurance company.

12. Under the required claim forms provision of a health insurance policy, a company must furnish the form to the insured within how many days after receiving a notice of claim?

    A. 10
    B. 15
    C. 21
    D. 30

13. Under what circumstances can a claim associated with a preexisting condition be denied, assuming the policy's contestable period has expired?

   A. Losses associated with preexisting conditions are permanently excluded; an associated claim would never be paid
   B. In the event the applicant concealed the condition and it was not noted on the application
   C. Losses associated with preexisting conditions are always covered, assuming the contestable period has expired
   D. In the event the condition has been specifically excluded from the policy, by name or description

14. Thomas, an insured, submits a claim and proof of loss for medical expenses covered by his major medical policy. According to the time of payment of claims provision, how soon must the company pay the claim?

   A. Immediately
   B. Within 30 days
   C. Within 90 days
   D. Within 150 days

15. Under the time of payment of claims provision, policies that provide for periodic payment of benefits (such as disability income policies) must pay such benefits at least

   A. quarterly
   B. monthly
   C. bimonthly
   D. semiannually

16. Which of the following statements pertaining to provisions in health insurance policies is CORRECT?

   A. The physical exam and autopsy provision entitles an insurance company, at the insured's expense, to conduct physical exams of the insured during a claim period.
   B. The change of occupation provision describes the changes the insured must make at his or her job to remain in compliance with the terms of a health or accident policy.
   C. The misstatement of age provision allows the insurer to adjust the benefits payable under the policy if the age of the insured was misstated when the policy was applied for.
   D. The legal action provision prohibits the insurer from taking legal action against the insured in a claim dispute until after 60 days from the time the claim was filed.

17. With what provision of a standard health insurance policy would the following clause be associated "The insured and the insurer shall have the same rights thereunder as they had under the policy immediately before the due date of the defaulted premium."

   A. Grace period provision
   B. Cancellation provision
   C. Reinstatement provision
   D. Time limit on certain defenses provision

18. Hubert, the insured, changes to a more hazardous job than the one he had when he applied for his disability income policy. According to the policy's change of occupation provision, what will happen when the insurer learns of his job change?

    A. A specified percent of benefits penalty will be charged against any future benefit payments.
    B. There is nothing the insurer can do as long as Hubert pays the premiums for the policy.
    C. Policy benefits will be reduced to an amount the premiums would have purchased originally based on the more hazardous occupation.
    D. The insurer will cancel the policy unless Hubert pays an additional premium to cover the higher risk.

19. Under the misstatement of age provision in a health insurance policy, what can a company do if it discovers that an insured gave a wrong age at the time of application?

    A. Cancel the policy
    B. Increase the premium
    C. Adjust the benefits
    D. Assess a penalty

20. According to the optional misstatement of age provision, all of the following statements are correct EXCEPT

    A. if the insured actually was younger at the time of application than shown in the policy, benefits would be increased
    B. if the insured actually was older at the time of application than shown in the policy, benefits would be reduced
    C. if the insured actually was older at the time of application than shown in the policy, the excess premiums paid would be refunded
    D. if the age of the insured is misstated at the time of application, all amounts payable under the policy would be what the premiums paid would have purchased at the correct age

21. The optional provision, "other insurance in this insurer," is specifically designed to

    A. limit the risk with any one individual insured by the company
    B. avoid issuing two policies on an insured person
    C. restrict an insured's coverage to one type of accident and health insurance
    D. discount the premiums if more than one policy is issued to insure the same individual

22. How does an insurer treat benefits that are payable for expenses incurred when the company accepted the risk without being notified of other existing coverage for the same risk?

    A. It deducts them.
    B. It estimates them.
    C. It prorates them.
    D. It eliminates them.

23. If total disability (loss-of-time) benefits from all disability income coverage for the same loss exceed the insured's monthly earnings at the time of disability, what is the insurer's liability to the insured?

    A. The insurer must pay the total benefits as specified in the policy.
    B. The insurer can cancel the policy, claiming overinsurance.
    C. The insurer must pay the proportionate amount of benefits that the insured's earnings bear to the total benefits.
    D. The insurer can reduce the benefits payable by half.

24. Naomi is killed in an auto accident before she is able to pay the semiannual $80 premium on her $30,000 accident policy. Under the policy's unpaid premium provision, her beneficiary will receive a check for

    A. $0
    B. $29,840
    C. $29,920
    D. $30,000

25. All of the following specify owners' rights in a health insurance policy EXCEPT

    A. unpaid premium provision
    B. incontestable provision
    C. grace period provision
    D. reinstatement provision

26. Under the standard cancellation provision, a company has the right to cancel a policy at any time with how many days written notice to the insured?

    A. 5 days
    B. 15 days
    C. 30 days
    D. 60 days

27. Any standard health insurance policy provision that is in conflict with a state statute

    A. is automatically amended to conform to the state statute
    B. is deleted entirely from the policy
    C. is kept in the policy verbatim, but with a rider added
    D. supersedes the statute, and remains in force

28. Under the optional illegal occupation provision, which of the following applies if a loss occurs while the insured is participating in a felony or an illegal occupation?

    A. The insured's policy is automatically canceled.
    B. The insurer is not liable for that specific loss.
    C. Benefits are reduced by an amount specified in the policy.
    D. The policy is voided, as if it were never issued.

29. The insurer under a health policy is liable for which of the following losses?

    A. Those sustained while under the influence of alcohol
    B. Those sustained while under the influence of an illegal narcotic
    C. Those sustained while under the influence of a prescribed medication
    D. Those sustained while committing a felony

30. A broad statement that generally appears on the first page of a health insurance policy and specifies conditions under which benefits will be paid is known as the

    A. assurance clause
    B. warranty provision
    C. insuring clause
    D. guaranty provision

31. All of the following statements apply to the insuring clause EXCEPT

    A. The clause identifies the insured and the insurer.
    B. The clause defines losses not covered by the policy.
    C. The clause usually specifies that the benefits are subject to all provisions and terms stated in the policy.
    D. The clause represents the insurer's promise to pay benefits for specific kinds of losses.

32. Which of the following words relates directly to the consideration clause?

    A. Endorsement
    B. Premium
    C. Exclusion
    D. Beneficiary

33. Concerning the consideration clause for a health insurance policy, all of the following statements are correct EXCEPT

    A. The consideration clause may specify the insured's right to renew the policy.
    B. Two principal elements of the consideration clause are the premium payment and the application.
    C. The amount and frequency of premium payment are stated in the consideration clause.
    D. A consideration clause may be included in a rider, if requested by the insured.

34. Generally, the consideration clause does all of the following EXCEPT

    A. lists the effective date of the contract
    B. defines the initial term of the policy
    C. lists the insured's beneficiaries
    D. states the amount of premium payments

35. After a health insurance policy is in force, the initial period of time that often must pass before a loss due to sickness can be covered is known as the

    A. probationary period
    B. trial term
    C. elimination period
    D. preexisting interval

36. The purpose of the probationary period is to

    A. provide a trial period of coverage for the insured at little cost
    B. limit the insurer's risk related to accidental injuries
    C. give the insured an opportunity to cancel the policy and obtain a refund if not entirely satisfied
    D. help the insurer to avoid paying benefits for losses due to illness contracted before the policy was issued

37. With disability income insurance, an elimination (waiting) period may NOT apply when the insured is disabled

    A. while at work
    B. by accidental injury
    C. while traveling
    D. by sickness

38. Elimination (waiting) periods in disability income policies are designed to

    A. eliminate claims for long-term disabilities
    B. last generally for one year
    C. help keep premium rates at a profitable level
    D. specify a limited period of time at the start of disability when benefits are not payable

39. Regarding the waiver of premium provision, all of the following statements are correct EXCEPT

    A. it is generally available with disability income policies
    B. the waiver may apply retroactively to the original date of disability following a waiting period
    C. such a waiver usually does not apply after the insured reaches age 60 or 65
    D. it is frequently included with both individual and group policies

40. Which of the following statements pertaining to the conversion privilege in group health insurance is CORRECT?

    A. To obtain a conversion policy an insured employee must show evidence of insurability.
    B. An insured employee who resigns or is terminated has up to one year to take out a conversion policy.
    C. During the period of time the insured is converting from the group to the individual plan, he or she is still insured.
    D. An insurer cannot change the premium amount for an insured who is converting to an individual policy.

41. All of the following statements pertaining to the conversion privilege in group health insurance policies are correct EXCEPT

    A. some states specify minimum benefits for conversion policies
    B. a conversion privilege applies when a group health policy is terminated
    C. insureds who resign or are terminated have 365 days in which to convert their coverage to individual policies
    D. an insured who is terminated from the plan can obtain a conversion policy without evidence of insurability within a specified period of time

42. Concerning the free-look provision, all of the following statements are correct EXCEPT

    A. most states require a free-look provision in health insurance policies
    B. it permits policyowners to return their policies within a specified time and receive full premium refunds.
    C. most states require a 30-day free-look provision in health insurance policies
    D. a policyowner does not need to give any reason for returning a policy in accordance with the provision

43. With an optionally renewable policy, the company reserves the right to

    A. cancel the policy anytime with five days' notice
    B. increase the premium on a policy if benefits paid to an insured exceed a stated amount
    C. modify the coverage if claims filed by the insured exceed an amount specified in the policy
    D. terminate coverage at any policy anniversary date or premium due date

44. Applicants for which of the following types of policies normally would require the MOST comprehensive underwriting?

    A. Basic medical expense insurance
    B. Industrial health insurance
    C. Limited accident insurance
    D. Guaranteed renewable disability income insurance

45. Which of the following types of health insurance policies prevents the company from changing the premium rate or modifying the coverage in any way?

    A. Optionally renewable
    B. Noncancelable
    C. Guaranteed renewable
    D. Cancelable

46. Which kind of health insurance policy assures renewability up to a specific age of the insured, although the company reserves the right to change the premium rate on a class basis?

    A. Noncancelable
    B. Guaranteed renewable
    C. Optionally renewable
    D. Cancelable

47. Which section of a health insurance policy specifies the conditions, times and circumstances under which the insured is NOT covered by the policy?

    A. Coinsurance provision
    B. Coverages
    C. Insuring clause
    D. Exclusions

48. Regarding preexisting conditions, the following statements are correct EXCEPT

    A. by most policy definitions, a preexisting condition is one that was contracted by the insured within one year before a policy is issued
    B. medical expense policies frequently exclude benefits for losses due to such conditions
    C. specifying exclusions for preexisting conditions helps an insurer to maintain reasonable premium rates
    D. disability income policies commonly include a probationary period to help control the risk of preexisting conditions

49. Exclusions for preexisting conditions help to avoid

    A. claims for long hospital confinements
    B. more complicated underwriting procedures
    C. adverse selection against a company
    D. insuring persons who are accident prone

50. If an individual health policy is renewable until the insured reaches age 65, when would the policy actually terminate?

    A. The first policy anniversary date which occurs on or before the insured's 65th birthday
    B. The first policy anniversary date which occurs on or after the insured's 65th birthday
    C. The day of the insured's 65th birthday
    D. December 31 of the year in which the insured turns 65 years old

51. Which of the following riders allows an insurer to provide a health insurance policy to an individual for coverage for everything but a certain injury or illness?

    A. Multiple indemnity
    B. Waiver for impairments
    C. Preexisting condition
    D. Optional exclusion

52. An accidental death and dismemberment (AD&D) policy paying twice the principal sum is known as

    A. a reimbursement policy
    B. double indemnity
    C. double consideration
    D. principal twice

53. For group health insurance, employees may be classified in all of the following ways EXCEPT by

    A. type of payroll
    B. duties
    C. length of service
    D. age

54. When an employer establishes a group health insurance plan, what evidence of insurance does each participating employee receive?

    A. Insurance notice
    B. Certificate of insurance
    C. Letter of confirmation
    D. Coverage form

55. Which of the following is a common feature of group major medical insurance?

    A. Double indemnity
    B. Dismemberment benefits
    C. Triple indemnity
    D. Conversion privilege

56. When a policy covers chemotherapy, cancer hormone treatments and other approved cancer treatments, benefits are available when treatment is received at all of the following EXCEPT

    A. through hospital inpatient treatment
    B. in a doctor's office
    C. through outpatient treatment at a hospital
    D. through a federally funded clinic

Answers & Rationale

1.   D.   A company may change the wording of a uniform policy provision in its health insurance policies once it receives state regulators' permission only if the provision, as changed, is not less favorable to the insured or beneficiaries.
QID: 1500

2.   D.   Individual health insurance contracts normally contain certain exclusions and coverage suspensions. These include losses associated with preexisting conditions (to protect the insurer against adverse selection); losses associated with deliberate acts of the insured, such as suicide and self-inflicted injuries; losses associated with excessive risk, such as hazardous occupations may entail; and losses covered by other types of insurance, to prevent duplication of benefits.
QID: 1501

3.   D.   Misstatement of age is an optional accident and health policy provision.
QID: 1502

4.   D.   Children of the insured are eligible for health insurance coverage until they attain the age of 19 or, if they remain in school, age 23. Coverage also ends upon the child's marriage.
QID: 1503

5.   D.   The change of occupation provision in health insurance is an optional, not required, provision. Nevertheless, many insurers include this provision in their disability income policies because an individual's occupation has a direct bearing on his or her risk profile and one's risk profile directly affects the premium charged.
QID: 1504

6.   D.   The entire contract in health insurance includes the policy itself, endorsements to the policy and riders attached to the policy. It protects the policyowner by stating that nothing outside of the contract can be considered part of the contract. It also assures the policyowner that no changes will be made to the contract after it has been issued, even if the insurer makes policy changes that affect all policy sales in the future.
QID: 1505

7.   C.   According to the time limit on certain defenses provision, the policy cannot be contested after two (or three) years for preexisting conditions unless the conditions were specifically excluded from the policy. A fraudulent statement on a health insurance application is grounds for contest at any time, unless the policy is guaranteed renewable, in which case it cannot be contested after the two or three year period expires.
QID: 1506

8.   C.   Under a health insurance policy's reinstatement terms, insured losses from sickness will not be covered unless they occur at least ten days after reinstatement. This is to prevent adverse selection against the insurer. Accidental injuries, however, are covered immediately.
QID: 1507

9.   C.   Depending on the state, the minimum grace periods that may be specified are typically seven days for policies with weekly premiums (such as industrial policies), ten days for policies with premiums payable on a monthly basis and 31 days for other policies. (Some states, however, require a standard grace period of 31 days, regardless of the frequency of premium payment or policy term.)
QID: 1508

10.   A.   Insured losses are covered immediately after a health policy is reinstated when the losses result from accidental injuries. Insured losses from sickness will not be covered unless they occur at least ten days after reinstatement. This is to prevent adverse selection against the insurer.
QID: 1509

11.   A.   Generally, a claimant must notify the insurance company within 20 days of an accident under a health insurance policy. Proof of loss must be submitted within 90 days of the loss, but if it is not reasonably possible for the insured to do so,

the deadline will be extended to one year. The company must supply its claim forms to the insured within 15 days of notice of a claim.
QID: 1510

12.   B.   Under the required claim forms provision of a health insurance policy, a company must furnish the form to the insured within 15 days after receiving notice of the claim. Otherwise, the claimant may submit proof of loss in any form that explains the occurrence, the character and extent of loss.
QID: 1511

13.   D.   A claim associated with a preexisting condition will be covered after the policy's contestable period (usually two or three years) has expired, unless that condition has been specifically excluded from the policy, by name or description.
QID: 1512

14.   A.   According to the time payment of claims provision of a major medical policy, the company must pay the claim immediately.
QID: 1513

15.   B.   The time of payment of claims provision allows for immediate payment of the claim after the insurer receives notification and proof of loss. If the policy provides for periodic payment of benefits (such as disability income policies), they must be paid at least monthly, if not more frequently as the policy may specify.
QID: 1514

16.   C.   Physical exams are conducted at the insurer's expense. The change of occupation provision describes changes that may be made to premium rates or benefits if the insured changes jobs. The legal action provision prevents the insured from taking legal action against the insurer any sooner than 60 days from the date the claim was filed.
QID: 1515

17.   C.   The reinstatement provision provides that when a policy lapses due to nonpayment of premium, but the insured subsequently pays the renewal premium (which the insurer accepts without requiring an application for a new policy), the policy will be reinstated with the same provisions and rights as before (with the exception of coverage for sickness-related losses within the first ten days after reinstatement.
QID: 1516

18.   C.   According to the policy's change of occupation provision, policy benefits will be reduced to an amount the premiums would have purchased originally based on the more hazardous occupation. Had Hubert changed to a less hazardous occupation (one that calls for a lower premium), the insurer would pay the full benefit for the loss and refund the excess premium to him.
QID: 1517

19.   C.   Under the misstatement of age provision in a health insurance policy, if a company discovers that an insured gave a wrong age at the time of application, it can adjust the benefits. Benefit amounts payable in such cases will be what the premiums paid would have purchased at the correct age.
QID: 1518

20.   C.   According to the optional misstatement of age provision, if the insured was actually older at the time of application than shown in the policy, benefits would be reduced accordingly.
QID: 1519

21.   A.   The optional provision, "other insurance in this insurer," is an overinsurance provision. It is designed to limit the company's risk with any one individual insured. An important consideration in health insurance underwriting is avoiding issuing a policy that provides too high a benefit, which would be a disincentive to return to work. Therefore, this provision sets a limit on the total indemnity for a particular type of coverage.
QID: 1520

22.   C.   Benefits payable for expenses incurred are prorated in cases where the company accepted the risk without being notified of other existing coverage. This limits overinsurance and is known as the "insurance with other insurers" provision.
QID: 1521

23.   C.   If total disability (loss of time) benefits from all disability income coverage for the same loss exceed the insured's monthly earnings at the time of disability, the insurer is liable for that proportionate amount of benefits as the insured's earnings bear to the total benefits. Total indemnities must be the lesser of $200 or total benefits under applicable coverage.
QID: 1522

24.   C.   Under a health insurance policy's unpaid premium provision, any due and unpaid premium (in this case, $80) is deducted from the settlement amount ($30,000). Therefore, Naomi's beneficiary will receive a check for $29,920.
QID: 1523

25.   A.   The unpaid premium provision of a health insurance policy does not pertain to owners' rights. It is designed to protect the rights of the insurer.
QID: 1524

26.   A.   Under the standard cancellation provision, the company has the right to cancel the policy at any time with five days' written notice to the insured. This provision is nevertheless prohibited in many states.
QID: 1525

27.   A.   In accordance with state regulation of the insurance industry, any health insurance policy provision that conflicts with state law is automatically amended to conform to the statute.
QID: 1526

28.   B.   Under the optional "illegal occupation provision," the insurer is not liable for any loss sustained from the insured's commission of a felony or engagement in an illegal occupation.
QID: 1527

29.   C.   Under a health insurance policy, the insurer is not liable for any loss attributable to the insured while under the influence of intoxicants, drugs or narcotics (unless such drugs were administered on the advice of a physician), or sustained while committing a felony.
QID: 1528

30.   C.   The insuring clause identifies the insurer and insured, specifies benefits and includes the insurer's promise to pay benefits for specific kinds of losses.
QID: 1529

31.   B.   Losses not covered by the policy would be listed as exclusions.
QID: 1530

32.   B.   The consideration clause describes the amount and frequency of the premium payments.
QID: 1531

33.   D.   The consideration clause is integral to a health insurance policy. As such, it would never be included in a rider.
QID: 1532

34.   C.   The consideration clause frequently lists the effective date of the contract, defines the initial term of the policy and states the amount of premium payments. In addition, it may specify the insured's right to renew the policy.
QID: 1533

35.   A.   The probationary period helps the insurer to avoid paying benefits for losses due to illness contracted before the policy was issued.
QID: 1534

36.   D.   The purpose of the probationary period is to help the insurer to avoid paying benefits for losses due to illness contracted before the policy was issued. Thus, many health insurance policies provide that benefits will not be paid due to any illness that commences during the first 30 days (or other specified period) following the issue date of the policy.
QID: 1535

37. B. With disability income insurance, an elimination (waiting) period may not apply when the insured is disabled by accidental injury. That is rarely the case with disability from sickness.
QID: 1536

38. D. Waiting periods in disability policies specify a limited period of time at the start of disability when benefits are not payable.
QID: 1537

39. D. A waiver of premium provision does not apply to group insurance.
QID: 1538

40. C. An insured employee who resigns or is terminated has 31 days to take out a conversion policy without having to show evidence of insurability. The insurer has the right to adjust the premium rate for the new policy. The insurance continues in force for the individual while he or she is converting from the group plan to an individual policy.
QID: 1539

41. C. Concerning the conversion privilege in group health insurance, an insured employee who resigns or is terminated has 31 days to take out a conversion policy without having to show evidence of insurability.
QID: 1540

42. C. Most health insurance policies contain a 10 or 20 day free-look provision. The common exception is Medicare supplement policies, which are required by state law to allow a 30-day free look period.
QID: 1541

43. D. With an optionally renewable policy, the company reserves the right to terminate coverage at any policy anniversary date or premium due date but may not exercise this right between such dates.
QID: 1542

44. D. Applicants for Noncancelable and guaranteed renewable disability income insurance would require the most comprehensive underwriting because they allow an insured's guaranteed renewal of the policy up to a certain age, without evidence of insurability.
QID: 1543

45. B. Noncancelable health insurance policies prevent the company from changing the premium rate or modifying the coverage in any way.
QID: 1544

46. B. Guaranteed renewable health insurance policies assure renewability up to a specific age of the insured, although the company reserves the right to change the premium rate on a class basis.
QID: 1545

47. D. The exclusions section of a health insurance policy specifies the conditions, times and circumstances under which the insured is not covered by the policy.
QID: 1546

48. A. A preexisting condition is one that first manifested or was treated within a stipulated period before the insured applied for the policy. This period is not necessarily limited to one year.
QID: 1547

49. C. Exclusions for preexisting conditions help to avoid adverse selection against a company by preventing those who are suffering from an existing illness from receiving benefits attributable to that illness.
QID: 1548

50. B. Policy terms are defined in terms of anniversaries, meaning the date of policy issue. If a policy defines its expiration date as the date the insured turns 65 years old, coverage would cease the first policy anniversary that occurs on or after the person's 65th birthday.
QID: 1549

51. B.   The waiver of impairments rider allows the insurer to provide a health insurance policy to an individual for coverage for everything but a certain specified injury or illness. This allows an otherwise uninsurable person to receive at least some amount of insurance.
QID: 1550

52. B.   An AD&D policy paying twice the principal sum if the insured dies as a result of an accident is known as a double indemnity policy.
QID: 1551

53. D.   Group health insurance participants may be classified by type of payroll, duties and length of service, but not by age.
QID: 1552

54. B.   When an employer establishes a group health insurance plan, each participating employee receives a certificate of insurance outlining coverage highlights. The employer, as policyowner, receives the master contract.
QID: 1553

55. D.   The double and triple indemnity and dismemberment provisions apply to accidental death and dismemberment (AD&D) policies, not to group major medical insurance policies. Group health plans allow insureds to convert to an individual medical expense policy with the same insurer if they leave their employment.
QID: 1554

56. D.   When an individual or group health insurance policy covers cancer chemotherapy and FDA-approved cancer hormone treatments and services, the covered individual must be entitled to benefits in any medically appropriate treatment setting.
QID: 1555

14

Disability Income Insurance

1. Which statement most accurately describes the purpose of disability income insurance?

   A. It reimburses the insured for covered medical and hospital expenses incurred due to a disability.
   B. It supplements disability payments from Social Security if those payments are less than $500 a month.
   C. It replaces a portion of the insured's income if he or she is unable to work due to a disability.
   D. It provides benefits to those who are not eligible for workers' compensation coverage.

2. From the insured's perspective, which of the following types of disability coverage would be the LEAST restrictive as to qualifying for benefit payments?

   A. Any occupation
   B. Own occupation
   C. Social Security
   D. Workers' compensation

3. Which of the following statements is CORRECT?

   A. Individual disability plans are only available on a short-term basis.
   B. Group disability plans are only available on a long-term basis.
   C. Disability income insurance benefits are paid out immediately following the disability.
   D. Disability income insurance does not provide a death benefit.

4. All of the following are common exclusions under a disability contract EXCEPT

   A. self-inflicted injuries
   B. preexisting conditions
   C. injuries suffered in the commission of a crime
   D. disabilities resulting from accidents

5. The amount of the benefit payable under a disability income contract is generally dependent on the applicant's

   A. age
   B. sex
   C. income
   D. education

6. Randy, an employee at a bank, earns $2,800 a month. He owns a disability policy that will pay him $400 a month. Believing he needs additional coverage, Randy applies for another disability policy from a company that has set a 70 percent of salary limit on the amount of disability coverage they will write. What is the monthly benefit that the company will issue on Randy?

   A. $1,960
   B. $1,560
   C. $1,160
   D. $400

7. Disability income benefits for partial disability typically are payable to eligible insureds for a maximum of

   A. one to three months
   B. three to six months
   C. one year
   D. two years

8. All of the following statements pertaining to disability income policies are correct EXCEPT

   A. Some policies use an "own occupation" definition of total disability.
   B. In some policies, the (residual) benefit payments are tied directly to the percentage of actual earnings lost.
   C. Benefits are payable as specified, weekly or monthly.
   D. Benefits may be payable for disabilities resulting from either accidental injury or sickness, and there are no exclusions.

9. Insurance companies control the benefits payable in their disability income policies by doing all of the following EXCEPT

   A. limiting the benefit amounts
   B. including elimination periods
   C. paying benefits in excess of the insured's income
   D. including probationary periods

10. All of the following statements pertaining to recurrent disabilities for disability income insurance are correct EXCEPT

    A. A recurrent disability is one that the insured experiences more than once.
    B. A recurrent disability policy provision would have no effect on the payment of benefits.
    C. A new elimination period may or may not be required for a recurrent disability.
    D. A recurrent disability may begin a new benefit period.

11. What is the initial period of time specified in a disability income policy that must pass, after a policy is in force, before a loss due to sickness can be covered?

    A. Preexisting term
    B. Probationary period
    C. Temporary interval
    D. Elimination period

12. All of the following statements pertaining to disability income insurance are correct EXCEPT

    A. The probationary period is an initial time specified to elapse after the policy is in force before the insured qualifies for sickness and accident benefits.
    B. Terry is disabled in a car accident that occurs six days after the issue date of his policy. The 15-day probationary period included in his policy would not affect the payment of benefits to him.
    C. Wanda's disability income policy has a two-year benefit period for total disability. She was in an auto accident and now is classified as partially disabled. She can expect to receive benefits for less than 2 years.
    D. Martin has disability income insurance that pays him $1,500 per month for 5 years if he becomes totally disabled. If he were to lose a hand in a mowing accident, his policy would not pay benefits for total disability.

13. In disability income insurance, an elimination period is a

    A. period of time when benefits being paid are temporarily discontinued to encourage the insured to return to work
    B. period of days following the start of disability during which benefits are not payable
    C. period of time preceding the benefit period in cases of disabilities caused by an accident rather than illness
    D. 30-day period following the end of a disability before benefits for a recurrent disability would be payable

14. All of the following statements apply to an elimination period EXCEPT

    A. The shorter the elimination period, the lower the premium for comparable disability benefits.
    B. Elimination periods reduce claims for short-term disabilities.
    C. Elimination periods usually range from one week to one year or longer, but most are at least 30 days.
    D. Depending on the policy, elimination periods may apply only to disabilities caused by sickness and not to disabilities caused by accident.

15. Durwood is hospitalized with leukemia and, upon checking his disability income policy, learns that he will not be eligible for benefits for at least 60 days. That would indicate his policy probably has a 60-day

    A. elimination period
    B. probationary period
    C. benefit period
    D. disability period

16. Which of the following terms best describes the maximum length of time that disability income benefits will be paid to the disabled insured?

    A. Coverage period
    B. Benefit period
    C. Disability period
    D. Elimination period

17. Benefit periods for short-term disability income policies typically vary from

    A. one to 12 months
    B. three months to three years
    C. six months to two years
    D. one to five years

18. Sidney makes $3,000 a month as a machine shop supervisor. His disability income policy provides for a monthly payment of $2,500 in the event of total disability. If Sidney were to become partially disabled, but continued to work at 60 percent of his pay, what would the policy pay, assuming it had a residual disability provision?

    A. $2,500 a month
    B. $1,200 a month
    C. $1,000 a month
    D. $0, since Sidney was not fully disabled

19. Which of the following terms relates to disability income insurance?

    A. Service basis
    B. First dollar
    C. Residual basis
    D. Coinsurance

20. What disability policy can be used to fund buy-sell agreements between partners or stockholders in a closely held corporation?

    A. Business overhead expense policy
    B. Disability buy-out policy
    C. Key-person disability policy
    D. Long-term care disability policy

21. What disability policy indemnifies the business for certain expenses incurred when the business owner is disabled?

    A. Business overhead expense policy
    B. Disability buy-out policy
    C. Cash value policy
    D. Key-person disability policy

22. All of the following statements pertaining to waiver of premium in health insurance policies are correct EXCEPT

    A. It exempts an insured from paying premiums during periods of permanent and total disability.
    B. It may be applied retroactively, after the insured has been disabled for a specified period.
    C. It applies only to a specified age, such as 60 or 65.
    D. It applies to both medical expense and disability income policies.

23. Which term BEST describes the policy provision for the payment of additional income when the insured is eligible for social insurance benefits but those benefits have not yet begun?

    A. Guaranteed insurability rider
    B. Cost-of-living adjustment rider
    C. Social Security rider
    D. Interim benefit rider

24. Which of the following statements BEST describes the purpose of key-person or key-executive disability insurance?

    A. It indemnifies the business to cover expenses and losses incurred when a key person is disabled.
    B. It provides tax-favored disability income benefits to a key person should he or she become disabled.
    C. It provides health benefits to a group of employees.
    D. It indemnifies the business to cover losses when an owner or partner dies.

25. A guaranteed insurability rider may be attached to which of the following policies?

    A. Disability income
    B. Medical expense
    C. Accidental death and dismemberment
    D. Group health

26. Which of the following riders provides for changes in the benefit payable based on changes in the Consumer Price Index?

    A. Guaranteed insurability rider
    B. Cost of living adjustment rider
    C. Social Security rider
    D. Payables rider

27. An eligible applicant for Social Security disability benefits must meet all of the following qualifications EXCEPT

    A. be under age 65
    B. enjoy a fully insured status under the Social Security program
    C. be unable to engage in gainful work for at least five months prior to the benefit payout
    D. have had surgery within 30 days before applying for benefits

28. To qualify for Social Security disability benefits, the disability must be the result of a medically determinable physical or mental impairment that can result in blindness, death or last at least

    A. 12 months
    B. 24 months
    C. 48 months
    D. 60 months or more

29. If a disabled worker who has collected Social Security disability benefits recovers and is then disabled again, must he or she incur another five-month waiting period?

    A. Yes, in every case.
    B. No, in no case.
    C. No, if the second disability occurs within five years.
    D. No, if the second disability occurs after five years.

30. An example of a state-administered disability program is

    A. Medicare
    B. Workers' compensation
    C. Medigap
    D. Social Security

31. All of the following statements are correct of workers' compensation insurance EXCEPT

    A. benefits are uniform throughout the states
    B. it pertains to work-related injuries or diseases
    C. employees do not contribute to the plan
    D. most laws permit the purchase of commercial workers' compensation insurance

32. When a group disability insurance plan is paid entirely by the employer, benefits paid to disabled employees are

    A. taxable income to the employee
    B. deductible income to the employee
    C. deductible income to the employer
    D. taxable income to the employer

Answers & Rationale

1. C. The purpose of disability income insurance is to replace a portion of the insured's earned income when he or she is disabled and unable to work.
QID: 1556

2. B. From the insured's perspective, qualifying for disability benefits would be at least restrictive under an "own occupation" policy, which requires that the insured be unable to work at his or her own occupation, because of a disabling sickness or injury, from any cause. Such a policy is more expensive and difficult to qualify for. An "any occupation" definition requires that the insured be unable to work at any job for which he or she is qualified; Social Security requires that the insured be unable to perform at any gainful employment; and workers' compensation provides benefits only if the individual is disabled because of employment-related injury or illness.
QID: 1557

3. D. Disability income insurance provides a periodic income in the event the insured cannot work due to a disability. No death benefits are provided. Both individual and group insured disability income plans are available on short-term and long-term bases, meaning how long benefits are payable. Short-term plans generally provide benefits for six months to two years; long-term plans provide benefits longer than two years, often until the insured reaches age 65. Disability income insurance benefits are paid out after an elimination, or waiting, period has been satisfied.
QID: 1558

4. D. Self-inflicted injuries, preexisting conditions and injuries suffered in the commission of a crime are common exclusions found in disability income insurance contracts.
QID: 1559

5. C. The amount of disability income protection a company will write on one individual is typically dependent on that person's salary or wages. For example, a person earning $2,000 a month may be limited by Company A to a monthly benefit of 60 percent of income or $1,200.
QID: 1560

6. B. Since Randy already has $400 a month in coverage, the company will issue no more than $1,560. The benefit from both companies would total $1,960, or 70 percent of Randy's salary.
QID: 1561

7. B. Disability income benefits for partial disability (an inability to perform one or more important job duties) typically are payable to eligible insureds for a maximum of three to six months.
QID: 1562

8. D. Disability income policies, like all insurance policies, have coverage exclusions.
QID: 1563

9. C. Insurance companies control the benefits payable in their disability income policies by limiting the benefit amounts, by including elimination periods and probationary periods and by specifying benefit periods. They do not want to pay benefits that would amount to more than what the insured actually earned before the disability.
QID: 1564

10. B. Policy provisions dealing with recurrent disabilities determine how and when benefits are payable.
QID: 1565

11. B. The probationary period is the initial period of time specified in a disability income policy that must pass, after a policy is in force, before a loss due to sickness can be covered. This provision is designed to protect the insurer against adverse selection.
QID: 1566

12.   A.   The probationary period in a disability income policy is the initial period of time that must pass before the insured qualifies for benefits due to sickness. The probationary period does not apply to benefits payable due to accidents.
QID: 1567

13.   B.   In disability income insurance, an elimination period is a period of days following the start of a disability during which time benefits are not payable. Elimination periods vary between one week and one year; the longer the elimination period, the smaller the premium.
QID: 1568

14.   A.   The longer the elimination period, the lower the premium for comparable disability benefits. An elimination period can be compared to a deductible since both are cost-sharing devices that can have a direct bearing on the amount of premium required of the policyowner.
QID: 1569

15.   A.   An elimination period is the time following an illness or disability during which benefits are not payable.
QID: 1570

16.   B.   The benefit period is the maximum length of time that disability income benefits will be paid to the disabled insured. The longer the benefit period, the higher the cost of the policy.
QID: 1571

17.   C.   Benefit periods for short-term disability income policies typically vary from six months to two years. In contrast, long-term disability policies carry benefit periods of two years and longer.
QID: 1572

18.   C.   A residual disability income policy ties the benefit payments directly to the proportion of actual earnings lost. In this problem, since Sidney is earning 60 percent of his predisability pay, the residual benefit would be 40 percent of the full benefit, or $1,000, calculated as .40 x $2,500.
QID: 1573

19.   C.   Disability income insurance contracts may be written on a residual basis, which means that they will provide benefits for loss of earnings without regard for occupational status and even if the insured is able to return to work on a full-time basis. The benefit is payable if the insured's earnings are reduced by a specified percentage below his or her predisability earnings.
QID: 1574

20.   B.   The disability buy-out policy is used to fund buy-sell agreements between partners or stockholders in a closely held corporation should a partner or stockholder become disabled.
QID: 1575

21.   A.   The business overhead expense policy indemnifies the business for certain expenses incurred when the business owner is disabled. These expenses, known as "overhead," include rents, utilities, and other similar expenses related to the daily operation of the business.
QID: 1576

22.   D.   The waiver of premium provision applies to disability income policies only.
QID: 1577

23.   C.   The Social Security rider, sometimes called the "social insurance substitute" rider, provides for the payment of additional income when the insured is eligible for social insurance benefits but those benefits have not yet begun, have been denied or have begun in an amount less than the benefit amount of the rider.
QID: 1578

24.   A.   The purpose of key-person disability insurance is to indemnify a business for expenses and losses incurred while a key employee is disabled; it does not benefit the key person. Typically, these expenses are those incurred while finding, hiring and training a replacement for the disabled key employee. As a disability policy, it insurers against disability, not death.
QID: 1579

25. A.   The guaranteed insurability rider may be attached only to a disability income policy. To qualify for the option, the insured must experience total disability for longer than a specified period.
QID: 1580

26. B.   The cost of living adjustment (COLA) rider allows for indexing the monthly or weekly benefit payable under a disability policy to changes in the Consumer Price Index.
QID: 1581

27. D.   An eligible applicant for Social Security disability benefits must be under age 65 (since all benefits paid after age 65 are classified as retirement benefits), enjoy a fully insured status and be unable to engage in gainful work for at least five months before the start of the benefits.
QID: 1582

28. A.   Disability under the Social Security program must be the result of medically determinable physical or mental impairment that can result in blindness, death or last at least 12 months.
QID: 1583

29. C.   If a disabled worker who has collected Social Security disability benefits recovers and is then disabled again within five years of the preceding disability, no waiting period is required.
QID: 1584

30. B.   Workers' compensation is an example of a state-administered disability program. Medicare is a federal social insurance program; Medigap is a type of insurance policy offered by commercial insurers. Social Security is a federally administered program providing retirement and disability benefits.
QID: 1585

31. A.   Workers' compensation insurance pertains to work-related injuries or diseases. Employees do not contribute to the plan. Most laws permit the purchase of commercial workers' compensation insurance. Workers' compensation benefits vary by state.
QID: 1586

32. A.   Disability benefit payments that are attributed to employee contributions are not taxable, but benefit payments that are attributed to employer contributions are taxable.
QID: 3347

Medical Expense Insurance

1. Fees for all of the following items typically are covered under a medical expense policy's miscellaneous expense benefit EXCEPT

   A. x-rays
   B. laboratory fees
   C. surgeon's fees
   D. use of the operating room

2. The miscellaneous medical expense benefit in a medical expense policy normally will cover

   A. physicians' bedside visits
   B. the administering of anesthesia
   C. drugs and medicine administered in the hospital
   D. room and board

3. Mark's medical expense policy states that it will pay a flat $75 per day for room and board for each day of hospitalization. The policy pays benefits on which basis?

   A. Indemnity
   B. Reimbursement
   C. Service
   D. Invoice

4. Margie's medical expense policy will pay for actual hospital room-and-board charges up to a stated maximum. Her policy pays benefits on which basis?

   A. Service
   B. Reimbursement
   C. Credit
   D. Indemnity

5. Wilbur's basic medical expense policy limits the miscellaneous expense benefit to 20 times the $90 daily room-and-board benefit. During his recent hospital stay, miscellaneous expenses totaled $2,100. How much of that amount will Wilbur have to pay?

   A. $0
   B. $210
   C. $300
   D. $2,100

6. Arthur incurs total hospital expenses of $8,300. His major medical policy includes a $500 deductible and an 80 percent/20 percent coinsurance feature. Assuming this is the first covered expense he incurs this year, how much will Arthur have to pay toward his hospital bill?

    A. $5,900
    B. $2,160
    C. $2,060
    D. $1,800

7. Major medical policies may include any of the following types of deductibles EXCEPT

    A. integrated
    B. flat
    C. corridor
    D. decreasing

8. When all or part of a deductible is absorbed by a basic medical expense policy, what kind of deductible is it?

    A. Decreasing
    B. Integrated
    C. First-dollar
    D. Corridor

9. The calendar year deductible provision of a major medical policy means that

    A. the deductible is applied against each claim during the first calendar year the policy is in effect
    B. all claims submitted during the calendar year are subject to the amount of the deductible
    C. the insurer pays a higher percentage of the medical expenses than the insured
    D. the deductible is applied only once during the calendar year

10. When separate deductibles are required for each illness or accident, what kind of deductible is in effect?

    A. Per cause
    B. Flat
    C. Per benefit
    D. Revolving

11. In major medical and comprehensive medical expense policies, a coinsurance provision

    A. helps to satisfy the deductible amount
    B. provides for percentage participation by the insured
    C. has no effect on claims
    D. does not apply until benefit amounts exceed $2,000

12. Major medical policies that pay 100 percent of covered expenses above a specified amount and after the insured's deductible contain what kind of a provision?

    A. Blue sky
    B. Maximum benefit
    C. Umbrella
    D. Stop-loss

13. Comprehensive medical expense insurance covers all of the following EXCEPT

    A. hospital room and board
    B. surgical fees
    C. hospital miscellaneous expenses
    D. loss of income due to sickness

14. Ralph incurs hospital expenses totaling $5,500. His major medical policy has a flat deductible amount of $300 and an 80 percent/20 percent coinsurance feature. All of the following statements pertaining to this situation are correct EXCEPT

    A. Ralph would pay the first $300
    B. his major medical would pay 80 percent of $5,200, or $4,160
    C. Ralph would also pay the balance of $1,040
    D. Ralph would pay $800, which is 20 percent of $5,500, minus $300

15. All of the following medical expenses generally are excluded from coverage under individual medical expense policies EXCEPT

    A. treatment for drug and alcohol abuse
    B. custodial care in a convalescent facility
    C. nursing care in a hospital
    D. nursing care at home

16. Which of the following methods of determining benefits under a surgical expense policy assigns a set of points to surgical procedures?

    A. Surgical schedule
    B. Reasonable and customary costs
    C. Corridor offset
    D. Relative value

17. Benefits paid for customary charges incurred during examination by an ophthalmologist or optometrist are included in

    A. disability income insurance
    B. surgical expense insurance
    C. vision care insurance
    D. basic physician's expense insurance

18. Which of the following statements regarding blanket health insurance is CORRECT?

    A. Benefits change as the group changes.
    B. Persons insured are named in the policy.
    C. It provides insurance for members of associations.
    D. It covers a group who may be exposed to the same risks.

19. All of the following statements pertaining to dental insurance are correct EXCEPT

    A. dental insurance generally is available in group plans, but seldom in individual policies
    B. a maximum dental benefit usually is specified for a calendar year
    C. dental coverage usually includes a deductible provision, but not a coinsurance feature
    D. benefits normally are payable for most dental work, including cleanings, fillings and extractions

20. What was the impact of the 1985 Consolidated Omnibus Budget Reconciliation Act (COBRA) on group health insurance plans?

    A. It requires any group health plan then in operation to cover all employees, without regard to years of service.
    B. It provides a tax deductibility for the cost of group health insurance coverage.
    C. It allows a group insurance participant to convert his or her coverage to an individual plan in the event of employment termination.
    D. It mandates that group health insurance coverage be extended for terminated employees for up to a specified period of time.

21. Which of the following policies pay a fixed hospital benefit directly to the insured, regardless of the actual hospital expenses incurred?

    A. Basic hospital
    B. Supplementary major medical
    C. Hospital indemnity
    D. Industrial health

22. Which of the following types of plans integrates its coverage with a basic medical expense coverage, providing benefits in excess of those specified in the basic plan?

    A. Supplementary major medical
    B. Comprehensive major medical
    C. Hospital indemnity
    D. Basic umbrella

23. Jane, an attorney, is eligible for medical expense coverage by virtue of her membership in the American Bar Association. She would be issued an individual policy at discounted rates. What kind of coverage is this?

    A. Group medical expense coverage
    B. Franchise medical expense coverage
    C. Blanket health coverage
    D. Industrial health coverage

24. Agnes purchases a round-trip travel accident policy at the airport before leaving on a business trip. Her policy would be which type of insurance?

    A. Limited risk
    B. Business overhead expense
    C. Credit accident and health
    D. Industrial health

25. An actress might insure her legs for a million dollars under what type of health policy?

    A. Franchise
    B. Limited risk
    C. All risk
    D. Special risk

26. A federal and state program designed to help needy persons, regardless of age, with medical coverage is called

    A. Medicare
    B. Medicaid
    C. Medigap
    D. workers' compensation

27. The purpose of medical expense insurance is

    A. to reimburse the insured for expenses incurred for medical care, hospital care and related services
    B. to provide periodic payments to an insured who is disabled and unable to work
    C. to pay for the recuperative or nursing care needed after a long illness
    D. to pay for the medical costs of injuries or disabilities contracted in the course of a worker's employment

28. A master policy is issued with each of the following forms of insurance EXCEPT

    A. franchise insurance
    B. blanket health insurance
    C. group disability income insurance
    D. group major medical insurance

Answers & Rationale

1.   C.   The miscellaneous expense benefit covers hospital "extras," such as x-rays, laboratory fees and use of the operating room. It does not cover a surgeon's fees, which would be covered under a surgical expense policy.
QID: 1587

2.   C.   The miscellaneous medical expense benefit in a medical expense policy normally will cover drugs and medicine administered in the hospital and other hospital "extras."
QID: 1588

3.   A.   Medical expense policies written on an indemnity basis pay a daily benefit for each day of hospitalization, regardless of the actual expenses.
QID: 1589

4.   B.   Medical expense policies written on a reimbursement basis pay for actual charges, such as room-and-board, up to a stated maximum.
QID: 1590

5.   C.   In this problem, the miscellaneous expense benefit limits payment to 20 times the $90 daily room and board benefit, or $1,800. Since the actual charges were $2,100, the insured must pay $300 (calculated as $2,100 - $1,800).
QID: 1591

6.   C.   Because this is the first covered expense Arthur has this year, he is responsible for the $500 deductible, and then 20 percent of the remaining costs. His share of the bill is computed as follows $8,300 - $500 = $7,800 x .20 = $1,560 + $500 = $2,060.
QID: 1592

7.   D.   Major medical deductibles may be integrated, flat or corridor, but not decreasing. Decreasing deductibles are related to life insurance.
QID: 1593

8.   B.   All or part of the integrated deductible is absorbed by, or integrated into, the basic medical expense policy; then major medical benefits are payable.
QID: 1594

9.   D.   A major medical policy's calendar year deductible means that when the deductible amount is met during the calendar year, all claims submitted will be treated for the balance of the year without meeting any new deductibles. Dividing the costs of medical expenses between the insured and insurer is know as percentage participation, or coinsurance.
QID: 1595

10.   A.   If a policy defines causes of loss as "each sickness or each injury," separate "per cause" deductibles must be satisfied every time a claim is submitted to the insurer.
QID: 1596

11.   B.   In major medical and comprehensive medical expense policies, a coinsurance provision provides for percentage participation by the insured. For example, a 75/25 coinsurance provision means the insurance company will cover 75 percent of the allowable medical expenses; the insured pays the remaining 25 percent. Coinsurance provisions apply after any required deductible has been paid.
QID: 1597

12.   D.   Some major medical policies contain a "stop-loss" provision, meaning that the insurer pays 100 percent of covered expenses after the insured's out-of-pocket payments for eligible expenses reach a specified level, such as $1,000 or $2,000. The definition of a stop-loss cap will depend on the policy.
QID: 1598

13.   D.   Comprehensive medical expense insurance covers room and board, surgical fees and hospital miscellaneous expenses up to a dollar limit.
QID: 1599

14. D.   The first three answer choices provide a good description of how coinsurance and flat deductibles work. Ralph pays the first $300 as a deductible; his major medical pays 80 percent of the remaining $5,200 amount, or $4,160; and Ralph pays the balance of $1,040.
QID: 1600

15. C.   Individual medical expense policies cover nursing care in a hospital, but usually exclude treatment for drug or alcohol abuse, custodial care in a convalescent home, and nursing care at home.
QID: 1601

16. D.   The relative value approach to determining benefits assigns a number of points to different surgical procedures, relative to the number of points assigned to a maximum procedure, such as a heart bypass. If a heart bypass were assigned, say, 1,000 points, every other procedure's point assignment would be relative to that. For example, an appendectomy might be assigned 200 points; setting a broken finger might be assigned five points. A dollar-per-point conversion factor is then applied to determine dollar benefits.
QID: 1602

17. C.   Vision care coverage, normally found in a group health insurance policy, usually pays for reasonable and customary charges incurred during eye examinations by ophthalmologists and optometrists.
QID: 1603

18. D.   Blanket health insurance covers a changing group of people who are classified as members of the group; they are not named individually. For example, a bus company may take out a blanket policy to cover its passengers. The benefits do not change as members of the group change.
QID: 1604

19. C.   Dental coverage usually features both a deductible and a coinsurance provision.
QID: 1605

20. D.   COBRA, which became law in 1985, requires employers with 20 or more employees to continue group medical expense coverage for terminated workers (as well as their spouses, ex-spouses and dependent children) for up to 18 to 36 months, depending on the event that led to the worker's termination from the group plan. The cost of the continued coverage is borne by the worker, not by the
QID: 1606

21. C.   A hospital indemnity policy pays benefits directly to the insured. These benefits are provided on a daily, weekly or monthly basis, for a specified amount, and are based on the number of days the insured is hospitalized.
QID: 1607

22. A.   A supplementary major medical plan is coordinated with a basic plan, designed to pick up where the basic plan leaves off. It covers expenses not included under a basic plan and provides coverage for expenses that are in excess of the basic plan's dollar limits.
QID: 1608

23. B.   A franchise health insurance plan offers health insurance coverages to members of an association or professional society. Individual policies are issued to individual members; the association or society simply "sponsors" the plan. Premium rates are usually discounted for such plans.
QID: 1609

24. A.   Limited risk policies provide coverage for specific kinds of accidents or illnesses. A traveler who purchases an accident policy at an airport would be covered in the event of an accident during that specific trip. The risk covered is limited to the trip.
QID: 1610

25. D.   Special risk policies cover unusual or extraordinary hazards not covered under ordinary health policies.
QID: 1611

26. B. Medicaid is a federal and state program designed to help provide needy persons, regardless of age, with medical coverage.
QID: 1612

27. A. Medical expense insurance reimburses insureds for expenses incurred for medical and hospital care, as well as related services. In contrast, the purpose of disability income insurance is to provide periodic payments to an insured who cannot work because of a disability. Long-term care insurance pays for rehabilitative or recupera-tive care needed after a long illness. Workers' compensation insurance pays for care related to a worker's injuries, disabilities or illness incurred on the job.
QID: 1613

28. A. Franchise insurance, although an alternative to group insurance, is not issued under a master policy. Rather, each insured person is issued an individual policy.
QID: 1614

16

Health Insurance Underwriting and Premiums

1. Major risk factors in health insurance underwriting include the following, EXCEPT

   A. physical condition
   B. lifestyle
   C. marital status
   D. occupation

2. Which of the following would be considered a moral hazard in underwriting a health insurance risk?

   A. Excessive drinking
   B. A serious heart ailment
   C. A hazardous occupation
   D. A family history of diabetes

3. Why are premium computations more complex for health insurance than for life insurance?

   A. Morbidity tables are constantly changing.
   B. The average claim is much smaller.
   C. Health insurance involves more than one type of benefit and claims are filed more frequently.
   D. Individuals are living longer.

4. Which of the following statements is CORRECT?

   A. Stan is a devoted hang-glider. His younger brother Kevin inherited his old equipment and took up the sport. Family history is considered a risk factor in insuring Kevin.
   B. Joyce's mother died ten years ago of cirrhosis of the liver when she was 58. Family history is a risk factor in insuring Joyce.
   C. Both Todd and his wife Joan are licensed but noncommercial airplane pilots. They do not have to identify their hobby when they apply for insurance.
   D. George's brother, his father and his father's father all had diabetes during their lifetimes. Family history will be considered a risk factor when George applies for insurance.

5. In health insurance underwriting, major risk factors include all of the following EXCEPT

   A. age of the proposed insured
   B. sex of the proposed insured
   C. type of residence of the proposed insured
   D. type of policy requested

6. All of the following statements pertaining to risk factors are correct EXCEPT

   A. Kimberly's job requires manual labor in a manufacturing plant. Betsy is an office supervisor who does no manual labor. Kimberly would probably be considered to have a higher disability risk than Betsy.
   B. Christopher, an office manager, would represent a lower disability risk to an insurance company than Ezekiel, a foreman in a farm equipment factory.
   C. Jill is 15 years younger than her supervisor, and as such, poses a higher risk to an insurance company.
   D. Men throughout their lives represent a higher risk than women to an insurer.

7. A primary consideration as to occupational risk in the underwriting of health insurance is

   A. length of employment
   B. type of employment
   C. past work experience
   D. financial history

8. Gene, Tom, Barry and Mark are all applicants for health insurance and each has a different occupation. The insurer has classified Gene's occupation as AAA, Tom's as AA, Barry's as B and Mark's as C. Based on this, which applicant poses the LEAST occupational risk to the insurer?

   A. Gene
   B. Tom
   C. Barry
   D. Mark

9. Kirk applies for a disability income policy. He notes on the application that he races cars on weekends as a hobby. Which of the following underwriting techniques would be considered illegal?

   A. Exclude any losses associated with Kirk's hobby from coverage
   B. Charge Kirk an extra premium and cover any losses associated with his hobby
   C. Refuse to issue a policy
   D. Force Kirk to change his hobby

10. Underwriting techniques commonly used by insurers in issuing policies to applicants who do not measure up to a standard rating include the following EXCEPT

    A. attaching an exclusion rider or waiver to a policy
    B. averaging total risks pending
    C. charging an extra premium
    D. limiting the type of policy

11. Which of the following statements concerning a coordination of benefits provision is CORRECT?

    A. This provision can be found in both group and individual policies.
    B. The purpose of the coordination of benefits provision is to avoid duplication of benefit payments and overinsurance.
    C. The provision allows all policies that cover an individual to divide equally all health care costs.
    D. Coordination of benefits provisions is found most often in family policies where the insured is still paying for a dependent's health care.

12. Individual health insurance policies usually are written on which basis?

    A. Participating
    B. Reserved
    C. Average
    D. Nonparticipating

13. With regard to substandard health insurance risks, which of the following statements is CORRECT?

   A. To provide coverage to substandard risks, insurers are allowed to charge an extra premium; however, they cannot alter benefit periods or waiting periods.
   B. An applicant can be deemed a substandard risk based on physical condition only; no other criteria may be considered.
   C. Because of stringent underwriting requirements, most health insurance applicants are classified as substandard risks.
   D. When the applicant represents a substandard risk, the policy may be modified to exclude a specific kind of sickness.

14. Which of the following statements concerning group health insurance plans is CORRECT?

   A. Experience-rated premium refunds are guaranteed.
   B. Group health insurance plans generally are nonparticipating.
   C. Plans issued by mutual companies usually provide for dividends.
   D. A group policy that is experience-rated does not make premium reductions retroactive.

15. In group health plans, if the plan is "noncontributory," the employer

   A. pays the entire premium
   B. pays none of the premium
   C. is allowed to select those employees who may participate in the plan
   D. must limit plan enrollment to five or fewer employees

16. With group health insurance, two major factors that influence dividends or experience-rating premium refunds are

   A. reserves and taxes
   B. competition and size of case
   C. expenses and claims costs
   D. type of employer and number of employees

17. What authority establishes the minimum number of persons to be insured under a group health insurance policy?

   A. Federal law
   B. The insurance company
   C. State law
   D. The employer

18. From an insurer's perspective, when a group is organized for some definite purpose other than to obtain group insurance, it is known as a

   A. natural group
   B. specific group
   C. blanket group
   D. contributory group

19. The effect of an impairment rider attached to a health insurance policy is to

   A. increase the premium rate charged
   B. decrease the amount of benefits provided
   C. exclude from coverage losses resulting from specified conditions
   D. lengthen the preexisting condition waiting period

20. With individual health insurance, all of the following would factor into the premium rate EXCEPT

   A. applicant's occupation
   B. insurer's reserves
   C. insurer's interest earnings
   D. insurer's expenses

21. Which of the following statements pertaining to health insurance benefits is CORRECT?

    A. Policyowners who have policies with identical benefits pay the same premiums.
    B. The greater a policy's benefits, the higher the premium.
    C. Policyowners who have the same jobs pay the same premiums.
    D. Premium amounts are determined only by the age of the insured.

22. All of the following statements regarding morbidity are correct EXCEPT

    A. morbidity tables are based on large numbers of persons
    B. morbidity is a major factor in premium calculations for health insurance.
    C. morbidity figures reveal when and how long an individual will be disabled
    D. morbidity statistics indicate the average number of persons at various age levels who are expected to become disabled each year

23. Brent is covered by his employer's group disability plan, which is noncontributory. He was involved in a car accident and was unable to work for six months. During that time, Brent received $9,000 in disability income payments. Based on these facts, which of the following statements is CORRECT?

    A. The disability income payments are not considered taxable income to Brent.
    B. Brent will be able to deduct the amount of premiums associated with his coverage, but will be taxed on the benefit payments.
    C. The disability income payments will be fully taxable to Brent.
    D. The disability benefit payments are deductible by Brent's employer.

24. The purpose of health experience tables is to

    A. indicate a health insurance applicant's chances of incurring a disability or illness, based on his or her past health experience
    B. provide an insurer with a record of all its insureds' medical histories
    C. allow an insurer to estimate the costs of future health claims by providing it with a record of average hospital, surgical and medical costs
    D. provide an insurer with a history of health claims submitted for a given geographical area

25. Which of the following statements regarding the tax treatment of disability premiums is CORRECT?

    A. Premiums paid for personal disability income insurance are deductible by the individual.
    B. Premiums paid by an employer for a group disability plan are considered a taxable benefit to the employee.
    C. Premiums paid by an employer for a group disability plan are deductible by the employer.
    D. Premiums paid by an employer are deductible by both the employer or the individual.

26. Rick, who has no health insurance, incurred $3,000 in medical expenses this year. Assuming his adjusted gross income was $29,000, how much of those medical expenses can he deduct from his income taxes, if any?

    A. $0
    B. $825
    C. $2,175
    D. $3,000

27. With regard to the tax treatment of medical expenses, which of the following statements is CORRECT?

   A. Personal medical and dental expenses reimbursed by insurance are not deductible.
   B. Unreimbursed medical and dental expenses are deductible by an individual taxpayer to the extent they exceed 15 percent of his or her adjusted gross income.
   C. Benefits received under an individual accident and health plan are taxable income to the recipient.
   D. Medical expenses, reimbursed or unreimbursed, are always deductible from an insured's income for taxation purposes.

28. Brian is self-employed and paid $3,000 for medical care, including premiums, in 2001. Which of the following statements is CORRECT?

   A. Brian may take a deduction only for the premiums he paid.
   B. Brian may take a deduction only for the medical expenses he incurred, excluding premiums.
   C. Brian may take a deduction for his medical costs to the extent they exceed 7.5 percent of his adjusted gross income.
   D. Brian may take a 60 percent deduction for the amounts paid for medical care, including premiums.

29. Mary worked at ABC Company and was covered by its health plan for 10 years. Three months before leaving ABC Company and starting a new job, Mary discovered that she had cancer. Which of the following statements about her new employer's health plan is CORRECT?

   A. It must cover all of her medical problems as soon as she enrolls in the plan.
   B. It must cover her medical problems after a nine-month exclusion period.
   C. It must cover her medical problems after a twelve-month exclusion period.
   D. It may deny coverage because of her preexisting condition.

Answers & Rationale

1. C. The major risk factors in health insurance are physical condition, moral hazards and occupation. Marital status is not a risk factor.
QID: 1615

2. A. Moral hazards are habits or lifestyles of applicants that could pose additional risk for the insurer. These hazards are evaluated carefully when underwriting health insurance policies.
QID: 1616

3. C. Premium computations are more complex for health insurance than for life insurance because the former involves more than one type of benefit and claims are filed more frequently.
QID: 1617

4. D. Family history is considered a health factor insofar as it relates to the health status of the living and the cause of the related deceased's death. Dangerous hobbies (such as hang-gliding or flying airplanes) is a risk factor, and must be disclosed when applying for insurance. Nonhereditary illnesses (such as cirrhosis of the liver) are not considered relevant for underwriting purposes.
QID: 1618

5. C. Health insurance underwriting addresses the age and sex of the applicant as well as the type of policy requested. The nature of the residence in which the proposed insured lives is irrelevant.
QID: 1619

6. C. A physical injury to a person who performs manual labor will incapacitate him or her longer than a person who does no manual labor. By the same reasoning, the nonmanual laborer (such as an office manager) represents a lower disability risk than a factory worker. Generally, an older applicant, not a younger one, is a higher risk to an insurance underwriter. Men are a lower risk

for disability than women only when men are younger. As they get older, men represent about the same level of risk as women.
QID: 1620

7. B. There are two major considerations regarding occupational risk when underwriting health insurance one is the probability of disability; the other is the average severity of disability. Thus, the type of employment one is engaged in and the classification it is given is very important.
QID: 1621

8. A. For health insurance underwriting, insurers classify occupations according to the risk they pose. The classes range from AAA, which include professional and office workers (the least hazardous occupations) to AA, A, B and C. Classifications of B or C indicate more hazardous jobs.
QID: 1622

9. D. An insurer could legally employ any of the techniques described in the first three answer choices when underwriting Kirk's policy. However, it is unlikely that Kirk would be denied coverage completely; one of the other options would probably be used.
QID: 1624

10. B. Underwriting techniques used by insurers in issuing policies to substandard risks include charging extra premiums to compensate for the additional risk, limiting coverage by excluding certain risks, and restricting or modifying the policy issued.
QID: 1625

11. B. The coordination of benefits provision is most appropriate for married couples, when both are covered by their employer group plan. This provision is found only in group plans. (Individual plans have a similar provision called a nonduplication of benefits provision.) It limits the total amount of claims paid from all insurers covering the patient. It prevents overinsurance and duplication of benefit payments. The provision establishes which plan is the primary plan, or the plan that is responsible for paying the full benefit amount. Once the primary plans has paid its full

promised benefit, the insured may submit the claim to the secondary provider for any additional benefits payable.
QID: 1626

12. D. Health insurance, like life insurance, can be issued on a participating or a nonparticipating basis. While most individual health insurance is nonparticipating, most group health insurance is participating, providing for dividend payments or experience-rated premium reductions if the insurer's expenses and claims are less than anticipated.
QID: 1627

13. D. Insurers are entitled to charge an extra premium, alter benefit periods or alter waiting periods in order to issue a policy to a substandard risk. An individual can be deemed a substandard risk based on physical condition, occupation or moral hazards. Only a small percentage of health insurance applicants are classified as substandard risks.
QID: 1628

14. C. Most group insurance plans are participating, meaning that, in some form, the group policyowner participates in any better-than-anticipated expense or claims experience. This form may be the payment of dividends (usually through mutual companies) or experience rating premium refunds (usually through stock companies). Dividend payments are never guaranteed but they usually apply whether or not the group policy is renewed. Premium refunds are not guaranteed and may be contingent upon policy renewal, but they can be applied retroactively.
QID: 1629

15. A. Noncontributory plans are so classified because the employer pays the entire premium. Covered employees do not contribute to the cost of the plan, although they may pay an extra premium to cover their dependents under the plan. Conversely, a contributory plan is one in which both employer and employee pay a portion of the premium.
QID: 1630

16. C. With group health insurance, two major factors that influence dividends or experience-rating refunds are expenses and claims costs.
QID: 1631

17. C. State law establishes the minimum number of persons to be insured under a group health insurance policy.
QID: 1632

18. A. When a group is organized for some definite purpose other than to obtain group insurance, it is called a "natural group," such as a company's employees or members of an association. Only natural groups may be insured under a group health plan.
QID: 1633

19. C. An exclusion or impairment rider rules out coverage for losses resulting from specified conditions, such as chronic conditions or physical impairments. By excluding such questionable risks, the insurer is able to issue a policy at standard rates.
QID: 1634

20. B. Health insurance premium factors include interest earnings, expenses, morbidity and for each individual insured, the type of policy being applied for, claims experience, age, sex, occupation and hobbies. Reserves are funds set aside by the insurer for the payment of future claims.
QID: 1635

21. B. With health insurance, the greater the benefits, the higher the premium. Policyowners who have identical policies with identical benefits will not necessarily pay the same premiums, since premiums are determined by a number of factors, such as age, sex and occupation.
QID: 1636

22. C. Morbidity figures in health insurance indicate the average annual number of disabilities or diseases at various ages. They are based on large numbers of people, and do not forecast an

individual's incidence or duration of disability. Morbidity is an important premium factor in health insurance.
QID: 1637

23. C. Disability benefits provided by a group insurance plan are fully taxable to the extent that they are paid for by the employer. In this case, since the plan was noncontributory and Brent paid nothing toward the premium, the benefits will be fully taxable to Brent. Had Brent contributed, say, 10 percent of the premium, then 10 percent of the benefits would have been received tax free. Disability benefits are received tax free in proportion to the premium paid.
QID: 1638

24. C. The purpose of health experience tables is to enable insurers to estimate the average amounts of future health insurance claims by providing average costs of hospital, surgical and medical expenses. These tables are adjusted periodically to reflect the most recent experience.
QID: 1639

25. C. Premiums paid by an employer for a group disability or sick-pay plan are deductible by the employer as a reasonable business expense. Premiums paid by an individual for a personal disability plan are not tax deductible; however, premiums paid on an individual's behalf by an employer under a group plan are not considered a taxable benefit.
QID: 1640

26. B. Incurred medical expenses that are not reimbursed by insurance may only be deducted to the extent they exceed 7.5 percent of the insured's adjusted gross income. An individual who has an adjusted gross income of $29,000 would be able to deduct only the amount of unreimbursed medical expenses over $2,175. Rick would be able to deduct $825. This figure is computed as follows $29,000 x .075 = $2,175; $3,000 - $2,175 = $825.
QID: 1641

27. A. Medical expenses that are reimbursed by insurance are not tax deductible. Unreimbursed medical and dental expenses are deductible to the extent they exceed 7.5 percent of an individual's adjusted gross income. Benefits received under an individual accident and health plan are not considered taxable income to the recipient.
QID: 1642

28. D. For self-employed individuals and their families, amounts paid for medical care, including premiums, are deductible, within limits. In 2001, self-employed individuals may exclude 60 percent of their medical expenses. This percentage increases to 70 percent in 2002, and rises to 100 percent in 2003 and thereafter.
QID: 3348

29. A. In the past, group health insurance plans typically excluded a person from coverage because of preexisting conditions. However, the exclusion for preexisting conditions is now limited to conditions for which medical treatment was received within the six-month period ending on the enrollment date. This exclusion period must also be reduced by one month for each month that the employee was covered at a previous job. Because Mary was covered by ABC Company's health plan for twelve straight months, the new plan cannot invoke the preexisting condition exclusion at all, and must cover her medical expenses as soon as she enrolls in the plan.
QID: 3349